User
Effective™
Buildings

User
Effective™
Buildings

Aardex Corporation
Denver, Colorado 303-987-9000
www.aardex.com

Acknowledgments

The contents of this book were researched, written, and designed with the assistance of Kim Long and the American Forecaster, Denver, Colorado.

The concepts and ideas represented here come from decades of successful achievement in the design/build industry. Aardex team members include: Richard "Rick" Butler (CEO), Jim Block, Hal Burwinkle, Chris Ernst, Michael Dick, Shane Fowler, Ed Gazvoda, Caleb Hebel, Brent Hockins, Skip Hohnhorst, Ric Johnsen, Willa Mandziuk, Glenn McWilliams, Scott Niebuhr, Cindy Russell, Kurt Schmidtke, Tara Tippett, Kyle Watts, and Ben Weeks.

Table of Contents

Introduction

To the majority of office workers, their work environments are nothing more than anonymous structures where employment happens. Most office buildings do nothing to improve morale or create a pride of place. At worst, those working in cubicles establish a dark, comic attitude toward their personal workspaces, regarding them as nothing more than cages separating mere employees from the ruling management class.

Have offices ever been more than this? A relatively recent arrival in terms of the history of architecture, office buildings were actually much worse environments one hundred years ago, and improved little until the last few decades.

If there is one defining characteristic that runs through this history, it is a differentiation between the private office and shared office space, most often representing a division of status and authority, with the private rooms usually representing the protected turf of executives and managers.

This remains a recognizable theme today, but there are strong forces at work altering how shared space is used, and the quality of the work environment in general. The biggest theme is density, how many workers there are per square foot of space, a concept driven by economics. Space costs money, and housing more workers in less space represents a simple equation involved with the cost of doing business. Spend less money, make more profits.

In the twenty-one years that the Aardex Corporation has been involved in the business of building offices, the theme of value dominates the plans of our clients. No matter the size of the organization, the economic factors that support the business activity require that money not be wasted, particularly on the real estate that houses it.

But our experience has also taught us that waste is not always obvious. Particularly in the last ten years, many of our projects have involved an increasing number of issues that have more to do with the quality and nature of the office space that is being built than the amount of floor space it contains.

Management in almost every type of organization is increasingly aware of the efficiency with which employees work, their job satisfaction, and the healthiness of the work environment. Employees who are hampered in performing their designated activities produce less work, requiring more workers — and a higher cost for labor — to maintain output. Conversely, employees who are supported in their activities and produce more work reduce the number of workers needed, and the amount of space needed to support them.

Consider the new US Forest Service Headquarters building in Albuquerque, New Mexico, which was completed in 2000. The output of this service-oriented organization increased while their number of people was reduced from 350 to 300. The cost of their space increased about $4.00 per square foot but their payroll was reduced about $45.00 per square foot. This is more than an eleven-to-one annual return on investment, not to mention the increase in output.

Job satisfaction, comfort zones, indoor air quality, control over privacy, noise levels, and other factors are part of this equation and all are fundamentally linked to the quality of the work-

---

The facts and conclusions found in this book depend heavily on decades of critical research conducted by dozens of key industry groups such as AIA, ASHRA, ASID, IFMA, IWSP, and NLB, as well as organizations such as Bosti Associates and the Rocky Mountain Institute. For a complete list of these resources, see page 184.

space and the functionality of the office building. The visual appeal of a building — on both the inside and outside — can also add to or detract from job satisfaction, contributing — or not — to the amount and quality of work performed.

Plus, productivity is directly influenced by *how* space is used. The proximity between team members, availability of meeting facilities, opportunities for casual interactions, and the distance between employees and shared equipment — all part of the layout of an office — can greatly enhance workflow and work output, or, if awkward and ill-conceived, greatly impede it.

From our increasing experience with these issues, Aardex has developed the concept of the User Effective™ workplace. Working closely with our clients, we help them recognize and design the physical elements of office space that are critical for being competitive and profitable in the modern economy. A User Effective™ workplace is custom designed, providing the right amount of space for the specific type of activities that will be performed there. User Effective™ workplaces are healthy environments, conserve energy, provide high quality ventilation and lighting, and are flexible, adapting to different needs as they arise.

Our research and experience emphasize how important affordability is to the bottom line; no matter how compelling building features may be, they must all represent a clearly defined return on investment. We believe that in the office environment, a custom-built structure must also provide a "return on people" in order to achieve long-term profitability.

This book represents some of the evidence we have gathered to support this policy. Whether or not it provides a convincing argument for you to work with us, we hope that it makes a difference, helping improve working conditions and the working environment.

The History of Office Buildings

"Firms and their managers must ensure that their employees will make creative contributions. They must first hire people with the potential for creativity and then they must structure their employees' environment in order to bring out this creative potential. Only by fostering the right people in the right place can creativity in organizations be maximized."

— Anne Cummings and Greg R. Oldham
(*California Management Review*)

Offices are not a modern invention. Long ago, commerce, religious groups, armies, and government bureaucracies created the need for clerical workers, record keepers, file managers, and other "pencil pushers" to deal with the information and paper documents that accompany such organizations.

This need dates back thousands of years, even before paper was invented. From papyrus scrolls to clay tablets, data management — not to mention filing and storage — created processes and problems that influenced the space in which such activities took place. Merchants were the first group to create a need for specialized office space, although churches and governments had their own requirements for locations where clerks and other workers could deal with the flow of documents.

During the 1400s and beyond in many major European cities, crowded conditions in central metropolitan areas produced a need for stand-alone buildings where merchants could conduct their business, which might include retail sales and warehousing along with clerical work. Up to that time, merchants typically worked and lived in the same buildings; this was the original version of work-at-home employment. In North America, the shift took a little longer, with New York City not experiencing such a shift until the late 1700s.

The English word office *has its origins in the ancient Roman empire. From a Latin root meaning "work" came the word* officium, *meaning "the performance of a task" or a "service." The English form as we know it today first appeared in the 1200s, but at this time it only referred to a position involving duties or authority, still one of its current uses. The meaning "place where business is transacted" first popped up about 1395 in* Canterbury Tales, *the classic book by Geoffrey Chaucer (1340–1400).*

Rapid expansions in a variety of industries triggered the development of large buildings in the 1800s, among them railroads, insurance, produce, oil, retailing, investment banking, and the telegraph. These expanding industries were using clerks in large numbers to handle orders, data, and files by the late 1800s. Some businesses in these areas had hundreds of clerks and a few employed one or more thousand such employees, with the office space necessary to house their activities.

In the U.S. the Census Bureau was reported to have almost 1,500 employees in Washington, D.C., by 1880; the Chicago, Burlington, and Quincy Railroad had about 300 employees when its new offices opened in Chicago in 1883; the Metropolitan Life Insurance Company had 500 clerks in one department alone in 1896 and 3,659 workers altogether at its headquarters in New York City in 1914.

14

In cities such as New York, the high price of land provided the incentive to expand buildings upwards, turning into the first "sky buildings" in the 1880s, limited to about ten stories until the wider availability of iron and steel — not to mention the elevator — enabled a rapid escalation upwards.

Companies such as Sears, Roebuck, located in Chicago, also had an incentive to create very large structures in order to keep up with their mushrooming success. In 1906, the Sears headquarters and mail order operations opened what was the largest building in the world at the time, a three million square foot edifice with plenty of room for large, open rooms filled with tables for hundreds of clerks, an expanding army of workers needed to keep up with the company's success.

This kind of open, shared office space existed long before cubicles. Dating back to the 1800s, many varieties of businesses grouped similar kinds of employees together in large spaces, with ranks and rows of desks forming neat grids. Most of the time, these desks were top-heavy with file racks or paper storage bins, giving workers some measure of privacy, shielded from the eyes of overseers and managers.

The modern office cubicle was invented about 1964 by Robert Propst, an industrial designer working for Herman Miller. Describing his motivation, Propst stated, "Today's office is a wasteland. It saps vitality, blocks talent, frustrates accomplishment. It is the daily scene of unfulfilled intentions and failed effort."

In 1915, the Equitable Assurance Company in New York City debuted the "Modern Efficiency Desk," the grandfather of the modern desk, as an adaptation for the open office system. The Efficiency Desk was a simple design with a flat top and a single rack of drawers below, deliberately created to allow managers easy visual access to the activity — or lack of it — of individual employees.

During this era, time and efficiency studies — pioneered in manufacturing operations — began to be applied to white-collar activities and these desks and the large open offices in which they were placed provided an ideal environment for turning paper pushing into regimented tasks. Following the lead of such efficiency experts as F. W. Taylor, who made a science out of time and motion studies in factories, office managers held a role similar to foremen and labor supervisors.

In these surroundings, managers played an active role as "big brother"; their active attention was believed to be a necessary part of office discipline and had a direct impact on how much work was accomplished. Workers who today complain about the lack of privacy in "cubicle farms" might gain some comfort comparing their current conditions to those of this era.

In 1964, Herman Miller, a major office furniture manufacturer, created the Action Office system in order to provide employees in uniform, crowded office environments with a flexible alternative, and one that provided more privacy. This

Cubicle Shrink

National surveys conduced by Haworth, Inc., indicate there has been a gradual reduction in cubicle size. Average size of cubicles in square feet:

	1985	2000
managers	115	64
technical workers	82	48
clerical workers	43	36

was the beginning of a more progressive attitude that gave more power and initiative to individual desk workers in order to alleviate the tediousness of their jobs; in this transitional period, tedium began to be linked to poor productivity. Some offices in Europe were also experimenting with this kind of open office redesign.

At Herman Miller, the development in this area is credited to Robert Propst (1923–2000), an industrial designer hired by the company to develop new kinds of furniture and provide better options for desk workers burdened by the impact of working in the open amid large groups of people. In his career, Propst is also credited with developing a quality control system for the production of concrete and an electronic tag identification system for cows, but his most notable achievement was the office cubicle.

> *"Cubicles don't kill productivity and morale — the poor use of cubicles does."*
>
> — Scott McMurray
> *(The Wall Street Journal)*

Propst reported that he first used the new cubicle concept for his own design team at Herman Miller, in an effort to help boost the team's creativity, improve interactive experiences among workers, and allow individual expression. "The last thing on the planet we'd ever have called it was the cubicle," he says. "What we wanted to control was relative enclosure. Over-cubiclized organizations were characterized by terrible communications, miserable relationships. And open space, with wild, bizarre intrusions on people, was also not satisfactory. We became interested in how you control privacy — privacy part of the time and access to each other part of the time."

His original vision permitted modular components to be used in variable configurations, allowing cubicles in the same space to vary in size and look, a deliberate attempt to bolster a sense of individuality and control. Herman Miller premiered the first cubicle components in 1968 based on Propst's efforts. The first Herman Miller cubicles had higher walls — six feet or more — than later models.

These days, an estimated 60 percent of the white-collar workforce — about 40 million adults — work in cubicles. Dilbert, the comic strip revolving around office cubicle lifestyles, debuted in 1989.

Why Build a New Building?

"Believe it or not, the place we work has a tremendous influence on the way we work. That makes the workplace an important strategic asset. It is an asset that can work to improve an organization's ability to create the sustainable resource we call intellectual capital." — Diane Turnwall (*Shoreline Business Monthly*)

Was there ever a period in the histories of major cities when every available office building was completely occupied? Possibly, if you consider the unique conditions during World War II, for instance, when almost all expansion was related to the war effort. Otherwise, the answer is no.

Depending on the year and the city, office vacancy rates have typically varied from a little less than 10 percent to more than 50 percent. Economic conditions expand and contract in perpetual cycles, producing shortages or surpluses of space, sometimes only locally but often over large regions. When the cycle is moving up, attitudes and investments favor building more space; the reverse is true in down periods.

Altogether, there are more than 12.8 billion square feet of office space in the United States (by the end of 2003). Every year, between 100 and 300 million square feet of new office space are constructed, ranging in size from small buildings with a few thousand square feet in area to those over 500,000 square feet.

Most of the time, it is difficult to match the supply of space with the demand. If all other factors were discounted, the

The Hidden Costs of Renovation

- Lease of space for temporary relocation.

- Disruption of normal activity if staff is not relocated.

- Health risks from construction activity.

- Temporary fixes for permanent problems (infrastructure will not meet future demands for communication systems, HVAC, handicapped access, etc.).

- Value of improvements may not benefit tenant (see page 22).

- Structural inadequacies limit ability to provide full range of available improvements.

- Structural inadequacies pose a barrier to improvements involving future building code changes.

- Sick building syndrome can not be completely cured, at least based on the current state of remediation.

organization anticipating a need to grow would benefit most by expanding during a period when there was a surplus of space available, a point when rates are usually low, the proverbial "buyers market." In an ideal world, developers would also be able to match supply with demand, anticipating the right time to build.

In the real world, however, timing rarely works in favor of the organization looking for new space. Other factors are involved, including expansion and contraction cycles within an industry, the availability of new technology, and demo-

The Hidden Costs of Leasing Existing Space

- How space is used is dictated by what is available, not staff needs.

- Flexibility is limited by space and design restrictions.

- Temporary fixes for permanent problems (infrastructure will not meet changing demands for communication systems, HVAC, handicapped access, etc.).

- Value of improvements may not benefit tenant (see page 22).

- Structural inadequacies limit ability to provide full range of available improvements.

- Structural inadequacies pose a barrier to improvements involving future building code changes.

- Sick building syndrome can not be completely cured, at least based on the current state of remediation.

graphic influences. Plus, the true cost of a move or expansion involves key elements other than the affordability and availability of space. When it's time to move, it's time to move.

The cost of a move is unavoidable and impacts not just the budget, but employee commutes, relationships with clients and markets, insurance, building inspectors, and commercial neighbors. It costs money to move office equipment, set up phone lines, and reprint business cards, to name a few of the red-ink issues involved. Whether the move is to a different existing structure or a new one, these fixed costs do not go away.

Top Ten Office Features

According to research by BOSTI (Buffalo Organization for Social and Technological Innovation), these are the top ten workplace characteristics with the greatest effect on individual and team performance:

1. Acoustic privacy
2. Support for meetings and spontaneous collaboration
3. Support for one-on-one meetings in individual workplaces
4. Support for administrative services and office chores
5. Sufficient storage for work-related material
6. Distraction-free group workspace
7. Break activity
8. Dedicated project rooms
9. Attention to ergonomics and physical comfort
10. Accommodation of technology

Fiscal concerns can force extreme measures, such as adapting an existing location for expanded uses or updating the decor and support systems to provide a more modern, efficient setting. Renovation of an existing space, however, also comes at a cost, not the least of which is the cost of a temporary move to accommodate construction activity. Even if adaptation can be done without this extreme expense, the costs add up, including the loss of work associated with disruptions to routines and work spaces.

Remodeling adds value to an existing building, but this may not benefit the tenant as much as the building owner. Even if remodeling specifically targets the needs of a current tenant, some or all of the long-term benefits may go to future tenants. And whatever the cost of a remodel, the same expenditure can produce stronger benefits if applied to a build-to-suit building rather than an existing structure because construction dollars typically go farther when building from scratch compared to alterations.

To be truly practical when planning changes to office space, an organization should balance the real cost of any option, including leasing space in another existing building or renovating an existing location. These costs should include the immediate expenditures as well as the long-term implications.

These days, an organization has a third option as well, the design and construction of a build-to-suit office building created for its own needs. A design/build option may involve the purchase of land and building by the prospective occupant, or a long-term lease. In general, the greatest short-term financial benefits will come from a lease.

Use of Office Space

- On average, office workers spend about 50 percent of their time during the workweek working at their own desks.

- On average, 42 percent of an office worker's day is spent standing.

- On average, the amount of time an office worker spends at meetings away from desks: 7 hours per week.

- On average, 57 percent of office workers report pressure to increase productivity because of downsizing.

- On average, 60 percent of office workers perform additional work at home.

[Workplace Index Survey, Steelcase/Opinion Research Corp., 2003]

The Build-to-Suit Advantage

Offices designed and built to match an organization's needs have key advantages, including:

- **Size**. The amount of space provided matches the amount of space needed.

- **Uniqueness**. The type of space provided matches the type of space needed.

- **Flexibility**. Current and future needs can be accommodated by incorporating flexibility into the infrastructure and general design.

- **Efficiency**. HVAC and other structural elements provide the latest, most efficient use of energy, delivered effectively to separate zones.

- **Health**. The latest construction materials, HVAC air filters and exchangers, and effective floor plans reduce or eliminate many current health problems that plague office tenants.

- **Safety**. A new building can take advantage of design and technology to help shield employees from outside threats, improving morale.

- **Comfort**. Few existing buildings can provide comparable quality when it comes to comfort, the ability to provide ideal working conditions for individual workers.

- **Achievement**. Offices, individual work spaces, and meeting areas become more effective tools when uniquely adapted to the needs of a specific organization. The result can be an increase in productivity, providing payback that more than offsets the cost of the structure.

An office building that is custom designed and built for a specific client provides unique advantages. Compared to some lease options with existing buildings, a build-to-suit structure will typically cost more up front, but long-term, the economic benefits are positive.

Some of this advantage is in direct cost savings. A new, high efficiency HVAC system, for example, may cost more up front but will typically pay for itself in a few years — or less — through reduced energy use.

Indirect savings are also tied to the same HVAC system. When the comfort level of individual workers is improved because of the advanced temperature and humidity controls that can now be employed, the result is a reduction in aggravation, complaints, and stress, factors linked to low productivity and absenteeism. This is not just a "grey area" for improvement; numerous studies conclude the inside environment is a major cause of worker discomfort, stress, and lost productivity.

The majority of companies and executives have at least some understanding of this concept. At least 75 percent of the senior executives at Fortune 1000 companies would give up personal offices in order to enhance productivity at their companies, according to a Hixson survey. And a survey from the American Society of Interior Designers reports that 93 per-

Direct medical costs paid by U.S. businesses due to indoor air quality: $15 billion per year.
[*American Journal of Medicine*]

Productivity losses in U.S. businesses due to indoor air quality: 60 million work days per year.
[U.S. Environmental Protection Agency]

cent of business decision makers believe that the design of their offices is important. Yet 65 percent of the senior executives at Fortune 1000 companies have no systems in place to measure ROI linked to office facilities or employee productivity (Hixson).

The office environment is not just a physical space in which business functions take place, it is a critical factor in how well employees conduct business. With the proper care in design, a User Effective™ building improves productivity and contributes to the growth and well-being of the enterprise housed within it.

Other elements also make a custom building ideal for future fiscal well-being. They include the ability to shuffle people and work spaces within departments, floors, and an entire structure. When appropriate design elements include the right kind

---

Office Tenants Rate the 10 Most Important Office Features

1. Rental rates.
2. Comfortable temperature.
3. Indoor air quality.
4. Acoustics and noise control.
5. Building management that delivers what is needed.
6. Maintenance quality.
7. Responsive building management.
8. Effective communications with building management.
9. Building appearance.
10. Operating expenses.

["What Office Tenants Want," Urban Land Institute/ Building Owners and Managers Association]

---

of communications channels, lighting fixtures, and access points, the space is more flexible, allowing the organization to make changes when necessary in response to the inevitable changes that characterize modern office processes.

Yet another issue complicating activity inside offices is "sick building syndrome." After years of struggling with this illusive problem, some employers are exasperated with the whole concept of the indoor environment. Some reports suggest that employees may suffer more from stress and the psychological work environment than any real health issues tied to structures. Stress and psychology do play a significant role in the effectiveness of organizations, but there are also real effects linked to indoor air quality, noise, mold, and other factors that exist because some buildings are old, built poorly, or inadequately maintained.

Top 10 Office Complaints

1. Temperature too cold.

2. Temperature too hot.

3. Poor janitorial service.

4. Not enough meeting rooms.

5. Not enough storage space at work stations.

6. Poor indoor air quality.

7. Lack of privacy at workstations or in the office.

8. Inadequate parking.

9. Problems with computers.

10. Too much noise.

[2003 Corporate Facility Monitor survey from the International Facility Management Association]

In many cases, specific elements of "sick building syndrome" can be identified and fixed. All it takes is money and time. But with the current state of remediation technology, some experts believe that the syndrome itself can not be completely eliminated. A better solution may be to start from scratch and create a healthy new building.

Employee safety and comfort are elements that can help attract and retain talent, as is the unique pride of place that comes with a new building. The new structure does not represent the shadow of a former occupant, but is a distinctive "home away from home."

"Make people more comfortable; they become happier, they work more efficiently, their bosses are happy, and their bosses' bosses are happier. And, if it looks good, then everyone is happy."

— Susan Boyle
(Buildings Magazine, 9-03)

Pride of place is entwined with employee morale and this — just as much as the physical elements that make a safe and healthy environment for work — has a direct impact on the bottom line.

Employees with high morale work harder, are more loyal, and take less time off from work, reducing the burden of absenteeism. Equally important, the higher the job satisfaction, the more likely an employee is to remain with their employer. This is especially critical as job retention is one of the strongest bottom line factors affecting profitability. The cost of hiring and training new employees is directly tied to the rate at which existing employees quit.

Buildings that promote high morale also make it easier to attract the best new employees, because comfortable, healthy working conditions rank high on the list of desirable features among those looking for employment. This may include the visual appeal of a building — such as its facade, entrance area, and surrounding site — but is primarily focused on the quality of the workspace environment.

Perhaps most important is the issue of productivity. A new, efficient building has a direct impact on how employees work. It allows them to work more effectively because the structure supports their efforts rather than hinders them. In effect, the build-to-suit concept helps promote achievement.

Job satisfaction and even happiness are pleasant concepts and, according to most indications, of concern to most business leaders. This concern is not a simple case of paternalism, but an awareness of the reaction of employees to poor working conditions: absenteeism.

Employees who miss work due to illness or other factors have a direct impact on the bottom line. Not only is their work not being done while they are absent, but other workers may have their normal work schedules disrupted. Plus, there are a variety of costs associated with absenteeism.

"The impact of poor indoor environmental quality on workers is estimated as high as billions of dollars a year nationwide. A slight increase in productivity, seen as decreased absenteeism or increased attentiveness, may be very cost-effective."
— U.S. Army Corps of Engineers ("Productivity and Indoor Environmental Conditions Research")

When illness or disability is involved, this may include medical payments or insurance premiums, co-pays, and deductibles. At certain times of the year, as during flu season, higher rates of absenteeism may be considered a "fact of life" because they are expected consequences of life in modern, busy societies.

On the other hand, absenteeism is also known to involve much more than straight-forward physical illness. Among the factors causing workers to shun their jobs are squabbles with co-workers, disagreements with management, and bitterness over forced changes.

Psychological conditions in the workplace can also increase stress; employees who are at odds with coworkers or their bosses are typically more stressed. One consequence may be an increase in complaints about physical factors, including noise, poor lighting conditions, bad indoor air quality, lack of parking spaces, and indoor temperatures that are too cold or hot. More stress equals more complaints.

"Office occupants' perceptions of their physical work environment are influenced by their total experience at work. ... Relations with coworkers and supervisors, interest in their jobs, and attitudes toward their organization affect occupants' perceptions."

— Stan Aronoff and Audrey Kaplan (Total Workplace Performance)

Office environments that provide comfortable work conditions add value to the work experience, according to many studies they improve employee morale and reduce an organization's rate of absenteeism. Direct causes of some health problems are specifically linked to the physical office environment, and changes or improvements that fix these reduce the absenteeism. Such factors are primarily tied to indoor air quality — mold, fumes, odors, etc.

This may even extend to the normal range of health problems that might otherwise push workers to stay home. That is, people who feel "under the weather" but still report to work may find the office environment makes the final decision for them. When the motivation is high, people are less likely to get sick.

It is not just absenteeism that is involved here, but overall employee turnover. When conditions are perennially bad, some workers do more than just stay home on and off, they quit. Turnover produces disruptions and involves costs that reduce productivity and impact profits.

Costs in both absenteeism and turnover include direct and indirect elements. A work position that is vacant, even for a day, can force other workers to assume additional workloads, delaying or stalling normal routines or the progress of a project. If other workers need to work overtime to make up for this loss, the cost can be directly attributed to the missing personnel.

Long term, organizations often develop staffing levels to include the expected constant of absenteeism and turnover. The total number of employees is inflated to deal with the expected fluctuations day-to-day in how many bodies there are available to handle the work load. When a company is able to reduce absenteeism and turnover, the total number of employees needed drops. A smaller staff reduces payroll, improves productivity, and boosts profitability.

Temporary workers may be brought in to deal with some staffing fluctuations, but the cost of this service is often higher than for full-time positions, not only because of administrative overhead but for staff time needed to bring new people up to speed. Filling vacant spots with permanent workers is also expensive. One estimate puts this cost at about 1 1/2 times the salary of the original position, and the time required for the replacement to reach full efficiency as a year or more. Direct costs include recruitment, relocation fees, and other HR costs and administrative overhead; indirect costs include the initial low productivity of a new hire, time required from other employees to work with the newbee, and possible resentment, resulting in lower productivity from those involved.

Better offices = happier employees = less absenteeism and turnover. And this means the office itself can yield a positive ROI.

> "The research shows that when done well, investments in facilities can yield returns on investments that contribute to the business bottom line. The workplace is a tool that when appropriately configured and designed to fit the people who work there and the work that they do, can yield direct and measurable impact on the performance and productivity of the entire organization."
>
> — Eric Teicholz (*Facility Design and Management Handbook*)

Why Build a New Building?

An office facility represents a small fraction of the cost of the personnel who work in it. Yet crowded or improperly used office space creates significant barriers to work, reducing productivity and adding to absenteeism, both adding to the cost of doing business.

Businesses often seek new space in order to have room to grow, to take advantage of a better location, or to leverage the best lease deals. Even small organizations, however, could be better off by moving into new office space that has been custom designed for their own needs.

The cost of a custom build-to-suit structure may exceed that of comparable existing leased space, but in both the long- and short-term, economic benefits usually favor the former. Customized space saves money because it provides a more efficient use of space and creates a work environment that improves productivity.

Space in existing buildings is almost always a compromise for effective use because of the difficulties in adjusting use needs to inflexible structural elements. Older buildings also fail to meet appropriate standards for energy use, indoor air quality, access, and other vital elements that impact performance.

Lighting and Illumination

"Light is an energy with profound biological and health consequences for human beings that extend far beyond the question of adequate illumination for visual acuity."

— Ossama A. Abdou (*Journal of Architectural Engineering*)

The quality and amount of light have a direct influence on the quality and quantity of work. This link was well-known long before the office environment was an issue. Factories were the initial arena for the study of work and light and sunlight was the resource most often sought after.

Before gas provided a practical alternative, factories were limited in size by their ability to provide individual workers with illumination adequate for the tasks they performed. Sunlight was the ideal and windows provided the access. To increase access to this natural resource, clerestory window designs were adapted from churches as factories mushroomed in size during the industrial revolution.

Albert Kahn, Henry Ford's chief architect, found new ways to add window area as Ford's new assembly lines extended the definition of "large" in factory structures. Along with record-setting production, Kahn's factory buildings also pushed the design envelope to take full advantage of natural light, not just to improve working conditions but to reduce dependence on gas and electric illumination alternatives, a key cost savings.

In the past century, however, the cost of electricity in North America has been relatively low, allowing building designers to use more and more electric lighting as a primary source in factories and offices. At the same time, the amount of window space relative to floor space has declined, a factor related to the expansion of high-rise office buildings and their unique structural ratios. Floor space generated income, influencing designers to develop buildings with more floor area at the expense of window access.

The modern office typically has window access only on its outer perimeter, and often this coveted territory is reserved for private offices. The walls that define these offices isolate the windows from the central space where most desk workers toil.

The light that illuminates the modern office is often generated entirely from incandescent, fluorescent, and HID (high intensity discharge) fixtures. Despite some advances in bulb design, all of these sources were implicated in the decline of the indoor lit environment. Incandescent sources generate excessive heat, often contributing to uncomfortable conditions. Even with the latest HVAC systems, much of the air circulation is directly related to the removal of this wasted energy.

Office Lights

Applications for lighting in office structures include:

- open spaces
- passageways
- tasks
- meeting areas
- design accents
- decoration
- security
- emergency use
- access
- reception
- signage
- parking

Fluorescent fixtures have their own problems. The chief complaint is the quality of the light they emit. Although they

Lighting Glossary

ambient lighting. General lighting intended to illuminate rooms or large areas.

brightness. The subjective or individual perception of the amount of light.

daylighting. The use of diffused sunlight to provide interior illumination, using windows or skylights.

diffuse reflection. Unwanted reflected images visible because of a lack of contrast on a VDT.

direct lighting. Light falling directly on an object or surface from a light source.

direct glare. Unwanted source of illumination directly in the field of view that interferes with the primary visual target.

disability glare. Extreme glare that blocks or masks the view of an image on a VDT or produces discomfort.

foot-candle (fc). A basic unit of illumination on a surface, equal to one lumen per square foot.

foot-lambert (fl). A basic unit of illumination reflected off a surface, equal to one lumen per square foot.

glare. An interfering light source that is more intense than the surrounding area, causing visual discomfort.

illumination (illuminance). The amount of light reaching a surface, measuring in foot-candles or lux.

indirect glare. Unwanted source of illumination caused by a reflection from a light source or lighted area.

indirect lighting. Light generated by bouncing or reflecting off surfaces before it reaches a surface.

lumen. A basic unit of illumination equivalent to the light emitted by one candle at its point of origin.

run cooler and use less energy than incandescent, fluorescent bulbs produce light that is uniformly disliked for its lack of natural feeling. Flicker is also an issue, as these fixtures traditionally have been prone to an annoying variation in their output. Some modern fluorescent designs reduce or eliminate the flicker effect, but the quality of the light is still an issue.

In most offices, the lights are overhead and designed to flood rooms with uniform illumination. However, whether incandescent or fluorescent, the result is often overkill, providing too much illumination and producing another unwanted side effect, glare.

Overhead lighting fixtures are mostly relics of an earlier era, when desk workers managed piles of paper or pounded on type-

---

luminance. The brightness of a surface generated by lighting sources.

luminance disparity. A contrast between the brightness of two lighted areas within a field of view.

lux. A basic unit of illumination on a surface, equal to one lumen per square meter.

solar heat gain. A measure of the heat produced by direct sunlight striking interior or exterior surfaces of a building.

specular reflection. Glare or reflection on a VDT caused by a light source behind the viewer.

task light. Direct light source used to illuminate a specific work site, such as a desktop.

uniform glare. Glare created by large areas of surfaces that are too brightly lit.

veiling reflection. A type of indirect or reflected glare caused by overhead light fixtures.

Light Expense

- In a typical office building, the cost of energy to provide interior illumination is often between 25 and 50 percent of all energy use.

- In federal offices, the annual cost of energy used for lighting is estimated at about $17 million.

- In general, the cost of electricity to provide light for one office worker is about $50 or less per year.

- Interior lighting demands vary during the day, with the highest use during the peak working hours. This coincides with the peak of energy use, when rates are highest. The most efficient lighting systems reduce a building's demand on the electrical grid and can be adjusted to reduce usage when necessary. Less demand overall reduces the need for more power plants.

- Most current office lighting systems provide the same quality and amount of illumination for all workspaces, regardless of the type of work done.

- Most current office lighting systems generate up to three times more illumination than is comfortable for working with computers.

- Lighting cost reduction efforts range from the use of replacement high-efficiency bulbs to the redesign of lighting systems to reduce light waste. Energy savings from these applications vary from 30 to 50 percent, not counting the additional reduction in cooling costs associated with a decline in the production of waste heat.

- Unified/automated lighting controls can reduce the use of energy for lighting by 20 to 50 percent.

writers. Most of the lights we depend on today were adequate for that use, if not ideal, because they were designed to provide the right amount of illumination for the surface of a paper document, allowing efficient reading or typing.

These days, however, almost all offices depend on computers as their main technology. But the typical office has a light system designed to make paper documents easy to use, not computers. The clarity of computer screens is less than optimum when overhead lights reflect and glare off their polished surfaces. Even with the use of special anti-glare screens, uniform overhead lighting can produce continual problems for those people who spend most of their time in front of computers.

Additionally, a piece of paper requires more light than a computer screen, because the VDT provides its own illumination. In most cases, the illumination that is ideal for paper is several times brighter than what is ideal for a VDT. This kind of over-lighting reduces the contrast of type and images on the computer screen, making it harder to read and use, increasing eyestrain, and producing fatigue. Workers that move between paper documents and VDTs get even more strain because of the extreme contrast between the two formats.

Case Study

Site. San Dimas facility, Southern California Edison.

Project. Redesign of lighting to reduce energy usage and improve task illumination.

Results. Replacement of the lighting fixtures reduced the amount of watts per square foot from 2.5 to 0.9, a drop of 64 percent. However, the replacement lights provided more light for specific work areas, even though the overall amount of light was reduced.

Light Pollution: Glare

Glare is defined as any area within the immediate field of view that is brighter than the surrounding area and is strong enough to cause discomfort. Glare can also be divided into two types, **discomfort glare** and **disability glare**. **Discomfort glare** does not alter or mask the image it interferes with, but, as the name suggests, causes discomfort because of its presence. **Disability glare** may not cause discomfort, but blocks or obscures an object or field of view.

The most common sources of glare in offices are overhead lights and walls and ceilings or other surfaces that are too brightly lit, causing them to be reflected on computer screens. Bright lights are more likely to cause glare than dimmer lights. As a general rule, the closer a light source is to the center of vision, the more likely it is to cause direct glare. The most common sources of direct glare in offices are ceiling lights and windows that are improperly shaded or screened.

Optometrists studying vision problems related to the workplace believe that reflected glare is the number one culprit. Glare also contributes to posture problems because workers often sit too close to the screen or at odd angles in an attempt to use their bodies to block an offending light source. A compounding factor comes from normal office traffic; the bodies of passing workers alternately block and unblock sources of glare, creating stressful variations on a work surface or VDT.

Workers who spend all or part of their time parked in front of computer screens complain of numerous problems related to their computer-related tasks. These include:

- headaches
- blurred vision
- eye coordination disorders
- double vision
- eye strain or "tired eyes"
- eyestrain
- difficulty focusing
- dry eyes
- burning sensations

Some workers also report other effects, such as muscle strain that comes from twisted postures attempting to reduce the unwanted effects of glare. The cumulative effect: stress.

Some of these symptoms may crop up with or without the added discomfort of bad lighting and some may be related to existing visual defects. Nevertheless, lighting provides both a critical focal point for improvement in the average office and a useful tool because it can be manipulated to improve working conditions associated with VDTs.

As many as two thirds of all office workers indicate lighting

Case Study

Site. Federal Building and Courthouse (San Diego, CA), built in 1976 and managed by the GSA.

Project. New lighting system to reduce electrical use.

Results. Annual savings in the cost of lighting were more than $229,000, with an additional drop of more than $50,000 because of the reduced demand for cooling. Productivity gains resulted in savings of $1.3 million per year, ranging from 3 to 15 percent increases in various areas of the facility. Estimated payback time: less than eight months (147 percent ROI).

problems give them major problems, and a similar portion list poor lighting as the number one or number two negative issue in the office environment. Some employers may dismiss this as just another area for worker complaints, but the problem has a more direct effect, on the bottom line.

As workers respond to poor lighting, their work suffers. Cornell University researched this issue and found that 24 percent of workers at one office facility had lost time at work due to factors involving vision. In total, this loss amounted to a 2 percent reduction in productivity per worker per year.

Another study, this one involving a Post Office facility, concluded that addressing lighting problems also has a direct impact on productivity. This facility replaced its existing direct lighting system with a more effective indirect system in order to reduce electricity usage. But productivity also benefited, with a 6 percent increase per year. The net result: the new system paid for itself in less than a year.

Sometimes, however, building owners or facility managers are short-sighted when they target lighting for energy savings. Not uncommon is the quick fix of unplugging fixtures or removing bulbs or ballasts. Fewer lights means less electricity

---

Case Study

Site. Control Data Corporation (Sunnyvale, CA)

Project. Installation of a new lighting system to reduce energy use and improve working conditions.

Results. Overall lighting and maintenance costs dropped by 60 percent, resulting in a payback of about two years. Viewed separately, savings from reduced downtime and input errors and increased productivity achieved payback in just one month.

Lighting Goals

- **Task illumination**. Effective work is linked to effective light. Lighting systems can be selected to match specific tasks, such as working at computers or meeting in small groups. The right type of light for one kind of work is often inappropriate for another.

- **Individual control**. The ability to control the light levels and placement in individual work spaces greatly improves the effectiveness of a work environment. Individual preferences vary.

- **Natural illumination**. Visual access to the outdoors greatly improves work satisfaction, but most people prefer to be shielded from direct sunlight. Effective use of daylight can lessen the use of indirect room lights, thus reducing energy bills, and it also has positive psychological effects.

- **Visual appeal**. Lighting can be used to create or improve the overall sense of design in a room or other area of a building. Tenants respond positively to buildings with supportive design characteristics.

- **Energy efficiency**. Effective light systems should be cost effective, reducing the use of electricity and extending the useful life of bulbs.

- **Integrated systems**. Buildings should have advanced, computerized control over lighting systems in order to take advantage of daily light cycles, occupancy loads, area usage, and other factors related to the cost of energy.

- **Maintenance**. Long-term effectiveness should include simple and affordable maintenance.

used, but it also reduces the illumination that may have a critical impact on employee performance.

The most effective strategy with office lighting is to gain energy efficiency but target productivity first. The reason is not just reducing employee complaints, but saving money. If an office consumes 70,000 kWh in electricity use per year for lighting, it would only save a few thousand dollars by cutting this usage 50 percent, a wildly optimistic target.

But if the same office improved the quality of its lighting system enough to improve the productivity by 1 percent, a very

---

Direct vs. Indirect

Lighting systems provide either direct or indirect illumination. As noted earlier, **Direct light** is distributed downward with no barriers or redirection between the source and illumination target. **Indirect light** is reflected or diffused between the source and the target. A baffle or reflector under an overhead bulb produces indirect light by bouncing it off the ceiling or other area.

In general, **direct overhead lights** cause more problems than they solve because the light is too harsh and focused, creating glare, shadows, and other kinds of visual interference on work surfaces.

Indirect lighting spreads light rather than focuses it, filling in shadows and providing a more pleasing, uniform effect. But poorly designed indirect lighting systems — especially if they are too bright — can produce diffuse reflections, offsetting their other advantages.

Lighting Factors

Natural light has a direct relationship with the physiology of the human body, the result of hundreds of thousands of years of adaptation to life under the sun through the seasons. Sunlight contributes to health and a lack of it can be harmful. At an extreme, some people suffer from SAD (Seasonal Affective Disorder) and may actually become depressed in seasons when the amount of natural light is reduced.

An estimated 5 percent of the population suffers from this syndrome, with another 10 to 20 percent thought to be partially affected. The farther north, the greater the percentage affected, and the older the person, the more likely it is to occur. More women than men are affected by SAD. Appropriate indoor illumination not only helps prevent SAD from occurring, but can be used as a remedy.

The circadian cycles — the internal biological clock that is associated with resting and active phases of a person's daily life — is also linked to the amount of illumination available. At different times during the day, varying light levels can enhance or depress the activity levels of an individual, corresponding to this natural rhythm.

Although too little light may contribute to drowsiness, too much light can also be a problem, producing stress through overstimulation. The longer the period of time that a person works in under- or over-illuminated conditions, the more likely they are to feel stressed.

Age is another biological issue related to light. As people age, they require more light, a factor related to the natural decline of vision with aging.

conservative target, the savings would easily represent ten times more than the 50 percent energy savings of the previous example. For every 100 employees making $25,000 per year, a 1 percent increase in productivity amounts to $25,000.

Employee attitudes and reactions to lighting also support the need to improve lighting. According to a national survey from Steelcase:

- 86 percent of workers report they would experience improved mood and levels of energy with a higher quality of lighting
- 75 percent report that productivity would improve
- 66 percent report their creativity would improve.

Case Study

Site. Main Post Office, Reno, Nevada.

Project. Redesign to reduce the use of electricity for interior lighting and provide other improvements to make the inside environment more comfortable and effective for those working in it.

Results. A lighting retrofit included a new ceiling; the combined effect provided a more uniform indirect light in place of the former direct lighting system. The result was an energy savings of about $22,400 a year. Combined with savings on maintenance and other factors associated with the improvements, the payback for the $300,000 remodel was less than six years. An even greater bonus was realized with an improvement in worker productivity directly associated with the improved lighting. As measured by the pieces of mail sorted per hour, this gain was estimated to be worth between $400,000 and $500,00 per year, a payback in less than nine months.

Visual Efficiency

The average 100 watt incandescent light bulb produces about 1600 lumens, a measure of the amount of light emitted by the bulb. When this light reaches a surface, its intensity is measured in footcandles, with the intensity directly related to the distance between the surface and the light source. The farther away from the source, the less light available.

The ideal illumination for visual efficiency is between 30 and 50 footcandles. Below this, what you can see may be reduced; above this level, little improvement is noted.

Workspace lighting criteria include three main factors:

1. **Horizontal illumination**. The amount and uniformity of light that reaches horizontal work surfaces.

2. **Vertical illumination**. The amount of light reaching vertical surfaces such as walls. The general rule: lower levels of lighting on walls reduces reflection and glare on horizontal work surfaces.

3. **Ceiling luminance uniformity**. The constancy of illumination across a ceiling. The general rule: the more uniform the ceiling light, the less reflection or glare on worksurfaces.

After the oil embargo began in 1973, the federal government, along with most sectors of the U.S. economy, searched for ways to cut back on energy use. At one Social Security Administration data processing center, this led to the disconnection of half of the fluorescent lighting fixtures, a quick fix for an existing building with few other options to reduce lighting costs.

The electricity usage and cost subsequently dropped by 50 percent, as expected, but employee output also suffered, which was not anticipated. The loss of light led to a 28 percent reduction in productivity, more than offsetting the energy savings.

According to an analysis of this action, the National Lighting Bureau calculated that in order to save $1 dollar in electricity, the Social Security center lost the equivalent of $250 dollars in worker production.

In older buildings, disconnecting fixtures may be the only adjustment possible, short or long term, because there is no affordable means to control the use of the lights in a more efficient way. But with a new building design, the right lighting

Case Study

Site. 12,775 square foot drafting room, Pennsylvania Power & Light (Allentown, PA).

Project. Redesign of the lighting system to conserve energy, improve the quality of illumination, and reduce glare from overhead fixtures.

Results. Overall lighting and maintenance costs were cut by 73 percent, resulting in a payback in just under eight years. Productivity increased by an estimated 7.5 percent, resulting in a separate, additional payback in 73 days.

systems can be selected and placed in the first place, providing the most cost-effective way to deliver illumination from the first day of occupancy. And long term, when changes in staffing or use of space alter the lighting needs, the original flexible system can be readjusted without appearing "penny wise and pound foolish."

Even with the most efficient office designs, some artificial sources of light will always be necessary. Improvements in both incandescent and fluorescent technology will provide higher quality illumination in the near future, allowing more light production for less energy cost. Because of the increasing interest in higher quality lighting systems, more products from competing companies can also be expected, driving down prices and improving the range of selections and technologies available. This is particularly true with compact fluorescent bulbs and halogen bulbs, both recent commercial introductions with a trend toward higher output, improved quality of light, and lower prices.

"... design and management of the physical work environment is a critical contributor to the performance and financial well-being of organizations. From seemingly minor elements, such as reducing glare, to major elements, such as the design or reconfiguration of entire buildings, the physical facility can either impede or enhance worker performance."
— Eric Teicholz
(Facility Design and Management Handbook)

Another promising technological trend is the commercialization of LED light sources. LEDs (light emitting diodes) have been around for decades, but in the last few years, new white-light versions have become available. So far, these are mostly used in applications requiring low levels of light, such as flashlights, signs, and signal equipment for vehicles.

Illumination Rules of Thumb

- typical general luminance in an open office environment: 100 foot candles

- typical luminance on the surface of a document from general office illumination: 85 foot lamberts

- typical luminance on the surface of a document from a task light: 200 foot lamberts

- typical luminance from a sunlit wall or window: 2,000 foot lamberts.

- typical luminance generated by a computer screen: 10 foot lamberts

- recommended luminance for work spaces with computer screens [ANSI]: 18 to 46 foot candles

- recommended maximum ratio for illumination between the surrounding area and a computer screen [IES]: 3 to 1.

- recommended for areas with high computer/low document use [ANSI/HFS]: 18–27 foot candles

- recommended for areas with high document/low computer use: 37–46 foot candles

- recommended for areas with medium computer/medium document use: 27–37 foot candles

Aging Eyes

As people grow older, most have increasing problems with vision. With the population of office employees also growing older — heavily influenced by the large number of Baby Boomers in the work force — lighting will become a more critical issue.

The following figures represent average near-point viewing distances (the shortest viewing distance at which an object appears in sharp focus).

age 16	3 inches
age 32	5 inches
age 44	10 inches
age 50	20 inches
age 60	40 inches

Higher output versions are on the way, which suggests they will be used for interior lighting as manufacturing processes yield lower prices. The advantages of LEDs as a light source are extremely long life, very low use of electricity, and almost no excess heat. The quality of the light produced is also comparable to that of incandescent bulbs, making these modern bulbs a potential replacement for fluorescent. Before they are perfected for overhead use, they will find widespread applications for other indoor uses, including signs.

EXECUTIVE SUMMARY
Lighting and Illumination

The lighting systems in most modern buildings depend on technology left over from the era when most office work involved printed documents. The same lights that provide effective illumination for documents, however, cause significant problems as illumination for information displayed on computer screens, the new dominant office format.

When properly applied, high quality lighting in offices can reduce the use of electricity as well as reduce the excess heat generated by the lighting process. With the right amount and quality of light — not to mention reduction or elimination of glare — productivity increases. Just as important, appropriate lighting that replaces older systems has a direct payback in reduced eye and health problems linked to bad lighting.

Most importantly, the relatively small expense that lighting represents can yield an enormous improvement in productivity.

Windows and Daylighting

*"The history of architecture is
the history of man's struggle for light
— the history of the window."*
— Mies van der Rohe (1886–1969)

Only a generation or two ago, offices without windows were almost unheard of. In fact, just about every kind of building used these traditional openings to supply fresh air and light to interiors. Windows still provide this essential function in homes, but in many office environments, they are a rare commodity.

What happened to change the status of windows is the cost of energy. As the cost of heating and cooling escalated, it gradually became more practical to seal off interiors from outside air. This became more urgent following the oil embargo crisis of the early 1970s, when building owners and tenants searched for quick ways to reduce their overhead in the wake of the unexpected spike in energy prices.

When windows were used, they were sealed, preventing building users from messing with the carefully controlled inside climate. This move also coincided with the growth in office size, underway since the early part of the 1900s, which reduced the number of windows relative to the number of people working inside a building. For many office buildings, this meant the majority of employees worked in windowless rooms or were located far from the nearest window.

Some real estate experts estimate windowless office space

Sunlight Factors

The amount of light available for illumination from natural sources in an internal space is produced by three major factors.

1. **Direct exposure**. The proportion of the open sky with a direct line of access to a specific window.

2. **External reflection**. Features of the landscape and nearby objects, including other buildings, which reflect light and contribute to the total amount of daylight available. In most sites in North America, this is a relatively small amount.

3. **Internal reflection**. Surfaces such as walls and ceilings — as well as fixtures designed to bounce or channel sunlight — alter the amount and quality of light available.

costs 10 to 20 percent less that comparable space with windows, but this does not include the effects of windows on productivity.

This design consideration is tilted strongly in favor of facility management, not only because of the perceived control over heating and cooling the indoor environment, but because of another tricky factor linked to glass: sunlight. Even though windows were invented and widely used for thousands of years just to provide access to this natural resource, the light provided by the sun has the unfortunate characteristic — at least to some — of varying in intensity throughout the day.

The angle of the sun and cloud cover are variables that alter the amount of light that can be provided from outdoors. Often times, there is no ideal level outside the extremes of too much or too little, the former requiring secondary sources of illumination and the latter creating glare. In general, direct sunlight is less desirable than skylight, which is natural light diffused by the atmosphere, reflection, or a mechanical filtering system.

The variance between too much sunlight and too little was the main reason offices and other work places were quick to adopt artificial lighting as it became available, first from gas and then electricity. During the last few decades of the 1900s, windows in office buildings were there more as an architectural statement than a practical resource.

Currently, however, windows are gaining renewed interest as an essential component for healthy office environments. In many cases, they are being added to improve both air circulation and lighting systems, but with appropriate changes to keep them from also being a nuisance or adding to the cost of energy usage.

The two biggest enemies are solar heat gain — the heating effect caused by sunlight striking interior surfaces — and

Sunlight Variables

Factors that affect the amount and quality of sunlight at a given site:

- latitude
- altitude
- seasonal changes
- air pollution
- humidity
- building orientation
- obstructions
- longitude
- cloud cover
- time of day
- microclimates
- building height
- landscaping

glare. Architects have provided successful solutions for both.

Unwanted heat gain can be largely controlled with the appropriate placement of window openings. Taking sun angles into account — including both daily and seasonal variations — the windows are designed to minimize the effects of rays striking them directly. Recessed window bays, overhanging eaves, and other exterior design features are employed for this purpose. Modern window glass also provides additional armor through the use of coatings and invisible screens that mask unwanted light elements.

"Not only do windows fulfill nonvisual functions (i.e., satisfy psychological and biological human needs), they also provide natural light and heat to an interior and thereby influence the energy performance of a building."

— Nancy Ruck
(*Building Design and Human Performance*)

Glare is also related to direct sunlight and can be minimized with the same techniques used to control heat gain. Secondary glare, however, can be a separate issue, as windows typically create a large area of brighter illumination even when the sun is not streaming directly through them. This kind of bright space, in contrast to less-brightly-lit interior areas, can contribute to unwelcome contrast and reflected glare.

But here, too, design elements can be employed to useful effect. This can include the placement and size of the windows themselves as well as the use of shades or screens that deploy under targeted conditions. Clerestory windows — those placed along a roof line or high above the field of view — can also be used to provide light without increasing glare.

Daylighting is part of a current trend that combines environmental issues — decreasing dependency on electricity for lighting — with an interest in improving the quality of the workspace — the value that a natural source of light has compared with electrically-generated light. Daylighting, however, does not necessarily involve sunlight. Sunlight and its problems, including heat gain and glare, are shunted aside in favor of the cooler colors and diffuse illumination that reflected rays provide.

Architects and engineers have access to numerous tools and methods for determining the amount and quality of sunlight available in a given location, as well as how the features of a building design will be affected by it. Longitude and latitude are primary variables because they have a direct affect from season to season on variations in the hours of daylight and varying angles of sunlight.

Other factors that are taken into account include seasonal variations in humidity, average cloud cover, seasonal climate characteristics, microclimates of specific areas, and known levels of air pollution (particles suspended in the air affect how sunlight is diffused). When it comes to buildings, a building in Washington, D.C., will have different requirements, advan-

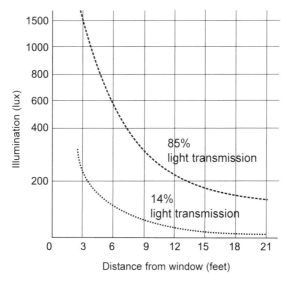

Skylight Illumination

Even without protective glazing, illumination from skylights drops off quickly with distance. [Adapted from Ruck Building Design and Human Performance, 1989]

tages, and disadvantages than a building in Portland, Oregon.

Harnessing sunlight for office illumination has a fundamental economic value. An estimated 50 percent of the energy used in North America for lighting is for commercial and industrial buildings; overall, lighting is responsible for 20 to 25 percent of total electrical usage. A reduction in energy used for lighting reduces the load on power plants and their fuel sources, reduces the amount of pollution produced in this process, and lessens the need for new plants and distribution systems to be built.

For one individual building, reduced use has a direct bottom line effect, lower electrical bills. And this advantage may soon be more than an interesting possibility in commercial environments. The American Society of Heating, Refrigerating, and Air-Conditioning Engineers Code and other professional sources have proposed a mandatory 25 percent reduction in electricity use for lighting, to be imposed at some point in the future. A few states, including California, Oregon, Texas, and Washington, have already adopted stringent new standards restricting energy use in offices. Clearly, the time has come to deal with alternatives to traditional interior lighting.

Economic factors linked to office lighting extend further. The type of lighting system used has an impact on the time spent on maintenance, the cost of replacement bulbs, and the amount of heat produced by light bulbs. With both traditional incandescent and fluorescent fixtures, the more light that is produced, the more heat is generated, requiring more energy to be spent removing excessive heat from work areas. These factors are all targets for reduction when appropriate access is made to sunlight.

Another trend in the building industry also points in this

> *"Companies should not consider the work environment as an afterthought. The physical work environment has to be entirely consistent with the strategic intent of the organization and the culture it is trying to create."*
>
> — Michael Bell
> Managing Director,
> Pricewaterhouse Corporate
> Real Estate Consulting
> Services Group

direction, the value of sustainability. Windows not only provide a direct element that can incorporate energy savings, but worth points on the U.S. Green Building Council's LEED™ rating system. (For more about the U.S. Green Building Council and the LEED™ system, see page 159).

To get daylight deep into building interiors without having it create problems, building designers also have additional tricks. Singly or in combination, these include reflectors and mirrors, skylights, light tubes (also known as light pipes), light shelves, fiber optic cables, lenses, prisms, opaque glass, automated blinds, and photo sensors, all designed and placed to provide access to sunlight — including into areas far away from windows themselves — while minimizing or eliminating the traditional negative effects.

In traditional building design, the rule of thumb holds that a useful amount of daylight extends into a room for a distance two to three times the height of the window through which it comes. This limitation is the target of the above technology

---

Case Study

Site. Engineering facility, Lockheed Corporation (Sunnyvale, CA)

Project. New building constructed in 1983 with specific features designed to increase the use of daylight without sacrificing working or heating conditions.

Results. Improvements related to daylighting cost an additional $2 million, but energy savings provided complete payback in about four years. An unplanned side effect was an increase in productivity due to a drop in absenteeism, down 15 percent, providing a 100 percent payback in one year.

---

and design applications. The goal: move more daylight farther into building interiors.

Some of the applications being used to do so are relatively new. Light tubes, for example, use the latest reflective foils or highly reflective paint to "pull" light down or across special flues. Such applications can direct natural light as much as 100 feet or more into windowless interior areas, even through multiple floors. Traditional atriums, skylights, and interior courtyards can also be added to building designs, helping put otherwise windowless areas in closer proximity to sources of sunlight.

Light shelves are horizontal design elements in window wells or window recesses. Such features bounce light up and away from the immediate zone near a window, spreading and diffusing it throughout an interior area.

Mechanized controls are increasingly being added to traditional window spaces, allowing more windows to be used without unwanted heat gain or glare. This kind of application couples motorized blinds or shades with photo sensors that react to the amount or angle of sunlight. Under preset conditions, the blinds partially or completely deploy, blocking direct rays from their interfering effects in side areas. Traditional exterior architectural features such as overhangs and eaves can also be employed to achieve this result.

"Modern buildings are often shaped with no concern for natural light — they depend almost entirely on artificial light. But buildings which displace natural light as the major source of illumination are not fit places to spend the day."

— Christopher Alexander (*A Pattern Language*)

Low-E Strategy

Window glass can be glazed to restrict the damaging effects of direct sunlight, including ultra-violet rays and solar heat gain. Traditionally, this involves the use of solar coatings, but this material has a downside. It also reflects or absorbs much of the visible spectrum, the component of this natural light that is most appreciated in interiors.

The solution is low-E glazing (low emittance glazing), a specialized coating type that blocks harmful UV rays and solar heat gain but allows most of the visible spectrum free passage. Low-E glazings are more expensive than other coatings, but provide the most desirable kind of light and can have a rapid payback. Because they allow a greater use of natural lighting, they reduce the use and cost of electricity for lighting. As an added bonus, they also have a higher R-value (insulation rating) than most other window glass, reducing the loss of heat generated by HVAC systems.

Low-e glass is being manufactured by more companies as the demand increases, providing a wider choice to developers and, more importantly, lowering the cost, down as much as 40 percent in the past five years.

Under control, daylight and windows have become new allies in the effort to create more comfortable office space. It is not just the light itself that is an issue, however, but the visual connection to the outside world provided by windows. It is no accident that in buildings where there is a mix of open spaces with cubicles and private offices, the private offices are the ones with windows and the executives or those in positions of power are the ones who are located there.

Other than providing a natural form of light for office interiors, windows provide a significant psychological impact on the work experience. Regardless of the view, the presence of windows keeps workspaces open to the world and less likely to be sensed as isolation chambers. And if windows provide a view of natural settings — woods, parks, or landscaping — there are additional benefits.

A study from the University of Michigan reported that offices with a view of nature provide a real asset in the interior work environment. Rachel Kaplan, a psychologist and author of the study, stated, "We found that the availability of

---

Window Dilemmas

In the modern era of office building design, windows are rarely intended to provide the major source of fresh air ventilation to the interior of a building. The problem with windows is they defeat the planned balance of ventilation, heating, and cooling that is provided by central HVAC systems.

Sealed windows provide important advantages:

- protection against external noise and air pollution

- uniform interior spaces that are more efficient to heat and cool

- elimination of radical changes in air flow and heating caused by proximity to open or closed windows

- elimination of disruptive wind gusts (typically more common above the fourth floor)

---

nature via a window strongly affected employee satisfaction, and the more natural elements they could see, the better. We also found that they had fewer headaches and felt generally more healthy."

Workers in these settings report less frustration, fewer physical problems, more patience with their work, and more enthusiasm on the job than workers in windowless rooms. The reasons for this effect are linked to a psychological benefit known as involuntary attention. Involuntary attention is a casual and infrequent view of something comforting — this can include a view of artwork or auditory exposure to music — that is not the main focus of attention or effort. Without such access, and particularly access to any windows at all, office work is more likely to include vulnerability to distractions and attention fatigue.

The Rocky Mountain Institute also has reported on the work benefits related to daylighting. According to their study of commercial buildings with this feature, absenteeism is reduced and work errors and defects drop when access to windows and natural sunlight is increased.

Not all studies show a direct relation between window

access and job performance, however. A major BOSTI research study showed a link between windows and job satisfaction but does not suggest that windows directly improve productivity.

On the other hand, most studies show that improvements in employee satisfaction itself is often tied to decreases in absenteeism and increases in performance. That is, satisfied workers are absent less and perform better. If windows improve satisfaction and this leads to an increase in performance, then they must be considered an important asset.

Private offices with windows have a traditional connection to job status, but the window itself may not be as critical as the private office itself. Windows are coveted and worth using as a perk because they are a valuable commodity, adding comfort and pleasure to the work environment. In the same BOSTI study that found no link to increased job performance, windows still rated high on a list of important office features, according to employee questionaires. Positive functions they attribute to windows include:

- counter-measure against feeling "closed in"
- providing sunlight
- providing a view of the outdoors
- illumination for workspaces
- visible indicator of weather and seasons
- a sense of connectedness to nature
- access to fresh air

The same workers, however, did not feel that the windows they had access to provided some of these features. Thus, even when windows are in place in some offices, their design may be deficient, a missed opportunity to improve the office environment.

More proof that sunlight has a beneficial effect comes from a recent study from the Heschong Mahone Group. Their research found that in retail stores, the addition of skylights prompted a 40 percent increase in sales. When classrooms were altered to provide more access to the sun, test scores increased between 20 and 26 percent.

> *"Windows that provide a view out, as well as daylight, can reduce stress and hence reduce the demand for health services. Daylight reduces the incidence of health problems caused by the rapid fluctuations in light output typical of electric lighting."*
> — "The Benefits of Daylight through Windows"
> (Lighting Research Center/
> Rensselaer Polytechnic Institute)

66

EXECUTIVE SUMMARY
Windows and Daylighting

Although the majority of office buildings have windows, the majority of office workers do not benefit from them. For many years, windows have suffered as expensive building features, subject to drafts, heat loss, and unwelcome glare.

A current trend revives interest in these old-fashioned features because, properly designed, they add a critical element to the quality of the work environment. The light provided by windows is a free natural commodity that boosts moods and energy, provides the most efficient type of illumination available, and helps workers who are cooped up in indoor enclosures benefit from visual exposure to the outside world.

The latest window technology also dramatically reduces the negative effects of direct sunlight at increasingly affordable prices.

Comfort Zones

"The simple premise behind the movement towards better working environments is that comfortable people are more productive. Comfort, however, is one of those catchwords that is easy to use and hard to define. People are comfortable when they feel comfortable, which is a state of mind dependent on both physical sensations and emotional states. Creating effective personal environments must account for both these elements together with the constraints of cost and technology."

— Wayne Morrow (Intellibuild 95)

Individuals have a wide range of reaction to temperature. What is comfortable for one person is uncomfortable to others and even the same person can experience shifting preferences over time, even during the same day. In the immediate area where an employee works, the temperature is often the most noticed — and complained about — factor related to the quality of an office environment.

The term "comfort zone" is defined as the range of temperature within which an individual feels neither too hot nor too cold. Several conditions make this a variable factor, not a constant. The most critical issue is individual preference, a complex variable influenced by genetics and personal backgrounds. Even within the same family, individuals react differently to temperature ranges only a few degrees apart; in an office where dozens or hundreds of individuals who are not related work in close proximity, such individual differences can result in permanent dissatisfaction, with some employees always out of favor with the prevailing indoor climate.

Comfort zones are also impacted by how the temperature is achieved. Radiant heat, for example, may be perceived as more comfortable to some individuals while forced air heat is more comfortable to others. Drafts which interrupt the standard delivery can compound discomfort, because moving air evaporates moisture from the skin, cooling the body. Humidity affects perceived temperature in a similar way, with lower humidity levels increasing the evaporative cooling and higher levels impeding it.

Secondary sources of heat can also cause discomfort, such as that produced by direct sunlight or radiation from a sun-warmed surface. Even when indoor air temperature is otherwise considered comfortable, such conditions are known to increase the perception of discomfort. The reverse condition, windows or walls that draw heat away from a room, can also generate perceived discomfort during cold weather.

"As far as I can tell, every office I've ever worked in, as well as every conference room I've ever visited, is either too hot or too cold. And they are hot and cold on random days."

— Lisa Belkin ("Life's Work," New York Times, 10/12/2003)

In general, people are also affected by color when it comes to perceiving heat or cold. "Hot" or "warm" colors — reds, oranges, yellows — tend to generate a perception of warmth and "cold" or "cool" colors — blues, greens — produce the opposite effect. In an office or industrial environment, color has been used to successfully moderate the comfort perception of the occupants, but some studies suggest this may only produce a minor and temporary effect.

No matter what the particulars are affecting an individual's comfort zone, it is clear that in offices, temperature is a major concern. In a recent survey of office workers from the

International Facility Management Association, the number one complaint was that the temperature was too cold. The number two complaint: the temperature was too hot. In another recent survey from the Urban Land Institute and the Building Owners and Managers Association, office tenants reported that a "comfortable" interior temperature was one of the most important features of a building, second in importance to rental rates; 95 percent rated this factor as "very important." The ability to control the temperature in specific suites and office areas is "very important" to 85 percent of those surveyed for this report. And yet another industry survey, this one from the Association of Interior Decorators, reported that office workers credit "good climate" and lighting above all other factors marking workplace value.

Air conditioning presents the same kind of variable. Individuals have different comfort zones for cool temperatures just as they do for warm, if not more so. Preferences in this area may be compounded by the period of time available for acclimatization to local conditions, the region where an individual was raised, family or group culture, the amount an individual is under- or

> *"As we well know, our skin doesn't always feel the same all over. Our upper body may be just the right temperature, but our feet are freezing. Our feet may feel fine, but our face is sweating. Any kind of uncomfortable information from our skin's thermal sensors can demand our attention. ... Being able to keep our temperature individually comfortable permits our attention to be invested elsewhere."*
>
> — Phyl Smith, Lynn Kearny (*Creating Workplaces Where People Can Think*)

Comfort Zone Rules of Thumb

- Women are more likely than men to respond negatively to temperatures that are too cool and to temperatures that fluctuate frequently.

- Occupants of smaller size (especially women) get chilled faster than larger occupants, and are more likely to respond negatively to temperatures that fluctuate frequently.

- Differences in clothing style between men's and women's wear varies the amount of insulation the clothing provides, affecting thermal perceptions.

- Different styles of office chairs — varying in insulation value — can affect the perception of temperature.

- For significant numbers of office workers, individual temperature preferences are more important to comfort than actual room temperature, an issue related to control.

- The more control individuals have over workspace temperature, the fewer the problems with indoor comfort.

- The slower the level of activity, the higher the temperature is preferred.

- The lower the temperature of the air in a ventilation system, the more likely it is to cause discomfort.

overweight, age, gender, time of day, whether the individual is a smoker or not, how recently a meal was consumed, the amount of sleep obtained the night before, the general state of health, humidity, the type of activity being performed, air movement, and other variables.

Personality traits also play a role here, because one individual may be naturally more inclined to adjust to prevailing conditions while another may not. Variations of only one or two degrees are typical in individual preferences, although some people have a much greater range of comfort. Studies have also shown that to maximize individual comfort zones, individuals should be able to adjust temperatures up or down by as much as 4 degrees F.

Even though this is an ideal adjustment range, the greater value may be in the act of control itself, not in the amount of variation it provides. At least one study has shown that workers report greater satisfaction with the indoor temperature when they perceive they can control it, even if the controls themselves do not actually change the temperature.

The problem for building owners and facility managers is that there is not a single temperature that suits every occupant. According to Michael Brill (*Using Office Design to Increase Productivity*), "Thermal comfort is *not* a 'best temperature.' Thermal comfort depends on the relation between the rate of heat production and dissipation, and is affected by ambient conditions such as temperature, humidity, and air motion and by the type and duration of activities people engage in, by the clothing they wear, and by their body type and size." In general, when the temperature is within an individual's comfort zone, they do not notice it, but the more it strays outside of this zone, the more they identify it as a problem.

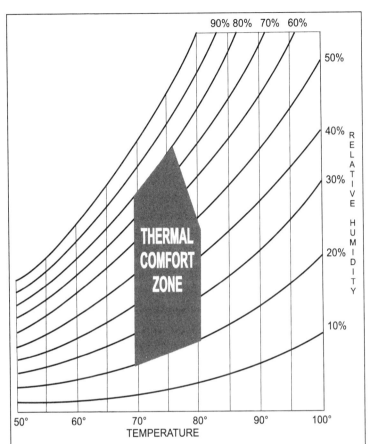

This chart indicates the relationship between temperature and relative humidity if there is no relative air motion. In general, the comfort zone would be skewed more to the left during the winter and to the right during the summer, not because of physiological differences from season to season, but because the average person dresses differently in winter than in summer, affecting how their body reacts to indoor temperatures. [Adapted from Fairey, Szokolay, and Auliciems]

However little or much individual preferences vary with temperature, the history of offices parallels efforts to provide the right comfort zone for workers. When the temperature is too hot or too cold, work performance suffers. In one recent study, for example, productivity at two telecommunications facilities were measured in comparison to variations in indoor temperature. When the air temperature was elevated beyond a certain point, productivity fell 5 to 7 percent.

Not only do temperatures outside the normal comfort zone affect performance, the more extreme the temperature, the greater the effect. Problems linked to excessively high temperatures include sleepiness, lack of energy, decreased performance levels, and increased error rates. Excessively low

Comfort Target

Target range for indoor air temperature in U.S. office buildings for typical desk-based activities:

Winter	68–75° F
Summer	73–79° F

These ASHRAE standards are based on 50% relative humidity indoors, air ventilation speed of 29 feet/minute, and normal weight seasonal clothing.

Relative Humidity	Winter	Summer
30%	68–77° F	73–81° F
40%	68–75° F	73–79° F
50%	68–75° F	73–79° F
60%	68–73° F	73–79° F

temperatures are linked to a reduction in alertness, restlessness, loss of concentration, and diminished performance on some kinds of mental tasks.

Excessive coolness has also been linked to cumulative trauma disorders in hands and arms. Excessive fluctuations in temperature can affect job satisfaction, which has an indirect connection to absenteeism. Overall, any continuing discomfort related to temperature adds to stress levels, which in turn increases health problems, absenteeism, and other manifestations of job dissatisfaction, including sensitivity to other physical factors such as air quality and noise levels.

Indoor temperatures that are outside an individual's comfort zone add to stress levels, contribute to job dissatisfaction, reduce alertness and concentration, sap energy levels, trigger absenteeism, and in general, reduce productivity.

Unwelcome temperatures are such a widespread fact of life in offices that most employees have learned to adapt to them. Dressing to accommodate the temperature is the standard response, with both clerical and managerial workers routinely stashing garments in their workspaces for anticipated bouts of discomfort. Typically, this means a sweater or jacket kept close to hand to deal with drafts or chills.

Yet another office tradition is just as commonplace: dueling thermostat settings. In this activity, discomforted workers routinely adjust a room thermostat up or down in an attempt to offset perceived problems. In many cases, facility managers have been drawn into this daily drama because they have to deal with consequences, typically temperature swings that are even more exaggerated. As a consequence, many modern offices lack thermostats to limit tinkering by occupants, or have tamper-proof room controls.

The movement of air provides yet another battle zone. Air vents are necessary even in offices heated by radiant heat because they provide a necessary source of ventilation. Yet whether heated or cooled, the air vents in most offices are a continuing source of vexation to individual employees because they create uneven flows of air, which parallels glare as an unwanted disruption to normal activity.

Traditional air vents provide little or no control by individuals in the path of their outflow. The result is a long-standing tradition of jury-rigged baffles and blocks, with books, files, cabinets, and other objects used to deflect or cut off the offending incoming streams. In some cases, occupants will use tape or cardboard to seal vents completely.

This kind of interaction has an immediate positive result for the person doing the interaction, but has negative results for a room in general. The only practical solution with both individual and group benefits is a system that allows individual preferences to be accommodated without altering the amount or quality of the air provided to the room. In many cases, this may not be economically or practically doable in an existing building, but can be incorporated into the initial design of an HVAC system in a build-to-suit building.

Even if productivity were unaffected by temperature, attitudes are not. As noted earlier, in recent surveys conducted by the International Facility Management Association, the number one and two complaints about offices are temperatures that are too cold and too hot, respectively. In the pioneering study of office productivity conducted by Michael Brill and BOSTI, about 25 percent of all office workers reported their

Humidity Rules of Thumb

Relative humidity is directly associated with human comfort. There is a range of individual comfort levels, and acclimatization to local conditions can also vary what is considered acceptable.

In most of North America, the normal range for humidity for building interiors is 40 to 60 percent, with 50 percent being average.

High humidity, from 70 to 100 percent, is directly linked to increases in:

- bacteria

- viruses

- fungi

- mites

- asthma

- allergic rhinitis

- interactions between chemicals

Low humidity, from 0 to 30 percent, is directly linked to an increase in:

- ozone production

- respiratory infections

- some types of bacteria, viruses, asthma, and allergic rhinitis are more prevalent at extremely low humidity

- dust mites

facilities were "too warm" and another 25 percent reported facilities were "too cool."

This study concluded that temperatures that were reported as too warm or too cool did not have an affect on bottom-line indicators of performance, but temperatures that fluctuated too frequently did. Other studies have concluded that while 80 percent of office workers rate thermal comfort as being "very important," only half think their own office systems provide a comfortable thermal environment.

> *"The ability to shape the work environment to one's choosing is a highly valued benefit. Individual environment control lies at the heart of most work setting preferences. People want to be able to control conditions in their physical work environment — to choose a comfortable temperature or suitable lighting, to shut out noise and visual distractions."*
>
> — Stan Aronoff, Audrey Kaplan (*Total Workplace Performance*)

This does not mean, however, that office HVAC systems are always to blame. Individual comfort zone preferences will likely always generate some complaints. According to ASHRAE (American Society of Heating, Refrigerating and Air-conditioning Engineers) guidelines, at least 5 percent of the occupants of a given office will always be dissatisfied despite the quality of the temperature control system, but the majority of complaints are directly caused by systems that do an inadequate job of heating or cooling.

Indoor air quality also involves humidity. Most people do not consider humidity to be an issue in office environments; they just take it for granted that it is maintained at an adequate level. But humidity, like temperature, has an affect on employees' satisfaction with the indoor environment and is linked to some health problems. Too much or not enough humidity will affect performance.

In indoor environments, the recommended target for relative humidity is 40 to 60 percent. Below 35 percent, low humidity levels are associated with health complaints such as dryness in eyes, noses, and mouths, and the lowest levels are implicated in the development of respiratory problems.

Office equipment is also affected by relative humidity. Low levels increase the amount of static electricity carried through rooms, posing a potential danger when people contact copy machines, fax machines, digital telephones, and computers. At the opposite range, too much humidity — typically more than 70 percent — triggers moisture condensation on interior and exterior surfaces of electronic equipment, potentially leading to electrical shorts and other malfunctions.

This excess moisture can also have a negative affect on humans in enclosed spaces. High humidity triggers the growth and spread of bacteria and mold, creating the risk of allergic reactions and exposure to disease.

Relative humidity is closely associated with comfort because the amount of moisture in the air relative to the temperature affects the amount of heat the human body dissipates through the skin. The lower the relative humidity, the more moisture evaporates from the skin, increasing the feeling of coolness. Relative humidity works in conjunction with air flow to produce this effect, as the movement of air also impacts how much moisture evaporates from the skin.

In general, when the temperature is high, most people feel more comfortable if the relative humidity is decreased, helping their bodies accommodate the heat. As a rule, a 10 percent increase in relative humidity makes air feel about 1 degree F warmer.

To date, most of the use of humidification systems in buildings has been with schools, art museums, libraries, high-tech manufacturing, and some corporate office headquarters. Because of the cost of adding humidification to HVAC systems, most small and mid-size office buildings have yet to upgrade equipment or to add this type of system by new construction.

Buildings not only have to accommodate the most desirable temperatures for the occupants, they have to feel accommodating to visitors, who are often not inside long enough to adjust to local conditions. In some modern facilities, lobby and reception areas are kept slightly warmer in summer and cooler in winter — typically 3 to 6 degrees F — to provide a more comfortable transition zone for visitors. An added bonus from this kind of zone control is a reduction in energy use.

Improvements in building performance for temperature control can be achieved even without the involvement of the HVAC system. Landscaping is a major target here. A single shade tree planted close enough to provide a building with protection from the sun reduces the need for air conditioning. By one estimate, one tree used in this application reduces the production of carbon dioxide ten times more than a tree planted in a forest because of the connection between shade and energy usage.

The quest to save energy has periodically been a major issue in office temperature control. During the energy crisis of the 1970s, both private sector and government organizations reacted to the steep increase in energy costs by altering the existing standards for internal building temperatures. What had previously been a relatively narrow range of settings — established to meet the comfort expectations of the greatest number of occupants — was expanded. In cooler weather, indoor temperatures were lowered to reduce the load on heating systems; in warmer weather, temperatures were boosted to provide a similar relief for cooling systems.

One of the larger temperature problems facing modern offices is the lack of control over conditions in individual workspaces. As the use of open office plans and cubicles has grown, so too has the adoption of broader, uniform temperatures throughout larger spaces, reducing the ability for individuals to control what works best for them.

System Failures

Factors related to poor heating and cooling performance in a building include:

- incorrect HVAC capacity (too much or too little)
- inadequate temperature controls
- inadequate, or lack of, zoning controls
- drafts and air leaks
- space usage that varies
- alterations to the building structure or envelope
- extreme variations in solar heat gain
- lack of outside ventilation
- variations in building occupancy

Office layouts also provide a variety of workspace placements, with some grouped together in interior masses and others arrayed along exterior walls or windows. Depending where a workspace is located, the control of the temperature can provide greater or lesser challenges to an HVAC system, as the proximity of windows, walls, and other workers increases or decreases the influences of other sources of heating and cooling. The affect of exterior windows and walls is the most obvious because of drafts, sunlight, and inadequate insulation.

The ideal office heating/cooling system would provide all employees with control over their own localized environment, whether in a cubicle or a private office. An under-floor ventilation system provides the most effective option, but this is also the most expensive system to design and install. In many cases, such an installation is too expensive, even given the potential for reduced energy use and improved productivity. A compromise system is a small-zone HVAC application, which provides controllable temperatures to a limited group of workspaces, typically 6-8 units at the smallest.

The type and placement of thermostats has a significant impact on office temperatures. In modern offices, the increasing use of personal computers, digital printers, fax machines, copiers, and other electronic devices adds heat to the indoor environment. The placement of a thermostat must take these heat sources into account and the unit itself must be monitored as the use of equipment changes in order to accommodate each added source of heat.

Modern HVAC systems can link individual thermostats to central computer controls, allowing automated programs to monitor and adjust the temperature in local zones. This kind of advanced building automation can provide a tremendous value in lowering energy use, and it also helps deal with the issue of occupant comfort. The cost of retrofitting these systems into older buildings, however, may decrease or even negate their potential value. For maximum effectiveness, HVAC automation should be part of new building design.

"For organizations, big or small, a 1 percent increase (or decrease) in productivity of core business operations, brought about by an inadequate workplace, is probably at least 10 times greater than a 1 percent increase (or decrease) in the value of the real property considered as a real estate asset."

— Federal facilities council staff
(*Learning from Our Buildings: A State-of-the-Practice Summary of Post-Occupancy Evaluation*, 2001)

EXECUTIVE SUMMARY
Comfort Zones

Many modern offices are a breeding ground of discontent because of uncomfortable working environments that result from outdated or ineffective heating and cooling systems. Although the majority of people agree on the same range of temperatures as an appropriate comfort zone, the two top complaints from office workers about their environment are "too cold" and "too hot."

Studies have shown that variations of only one or two degrees make the difference between one person's comfort and another's discomfort. Furthermore, most studies on the subject indicate a connection between a person's ability to control their own environment and their job satisfaction. Job satisfaction matters a great deal because it is closely linked to productivity.

The ideal solution: individual temperature controls for each employee. This may not be cost effective — it is almost certainly not possible as a retrofit goal for existing buildings — but a variety of options are applicable for build-to-suit projects.

Indoor Air Quality and Health

"Though many nonoffice workplaces pose far greater risks, the health concerns associated with an office setting are involuntary risks. Occupants perceive them to be human-produced, preventable risks that a workplace should not impose."

— Stan Aronoff and Audrey Kaplan
(Total Workplace Performance)

As long as humans have lived or worked in buildings, there have likely been negative health factors related to buildings. Imagine what it must have been like to work in a stuffy, enclosed room heated by a wood or coal stove and lit by kerosene lamps or candles. Even though these conditions must have produced contaminated air and those who worked there may have suffered from these conditions, they represented the norm for the period.

Some historians believe that the first rules governing ventilation for buildings date to the early 1600s in England. At that time, the king established a standard for ceiling height — at least 10 feet — and window dimensions — height greater than width. Both rules had one objective, to improve air flow in rooms so that smoke from open fireplaces would be less of a problem for occupants.

The first standards relating to the amount of air needed by a human to sustain life are thought to date to the mid-1800s, the result of research to determine how to keep miners alive in their unique enclosed environments. By the end of the 1800s, such concerns had advanced to include carbon dioxide levels and other toxic components of air. The earliest recommendations for airflow in buildings were based on these calculations, as well as efforts to minimize the spread of diseases.

In the first few eras of office building use, however, the goal of ventilation extended even further. In the days before daily showers were a common practice for American consumers, dealing with the body odor generated in crowded indoor envi-

Ventilation Health Factors

Negative factors linked to low ventilation:

- increased levels of carbon monoxide
- increased growth of molds and fungi
- build-up of fumes from paint, carpet, cleaning materials
- asthmatic reactions
- allergic reactions
- employee fatigue

Negative factors linked to antiquated or poorly-designed ventilation systems:

- introduction of vehicle exhaust fumes into buildings
- uneven circulation of fresh air
- extreme or uneven levels of temperature
- excessive use of energy
- undependable output
- increased failure rates during periods of temperature extremes

Components of indoor air environments associated with negative health risks:

radon	asbestos
carbon monoxide	cigarette smoke
lead	electro-magnetic-fields
VDT radiation	ozone
mold	cleaning solvents
dust	allergens
fiberglass particles	formaldehyde
nitrogen oxides	dry-cleaning residue on clothes
perfumes	other personal care products

VOCs (ethylbenzene, xylenes, styrene, and others)

Health factors related to the quality of the indoor environment:

headaches, dizziness, chest pains, eye irritation

infectious diseases

allergies

asthma

fatigue

loss of concentration

multiple chemical sensitivity (MCS)

sick building syndrome (SBS)

building related illness (BRI)

acute respiratory disease (ARD)

Air Pollution Characteristics

solids   dust, toxic particles, lint, mists, pollen, plant spores, and micro-organisms, which can be either visible or microscopic in size. Common sources of indoor air solids include minerals, plants, and animals (particulates from hair, feathers, fur, wool, or skin). Interior dust is created and distributed by normal activity, such as walking or using work surfaces. Other typical sources include maintenance and janitorial activity and ventilation from exterior areas. Liquid droplets are considered solids, although they are up to 100 times smaller than the particles that constitute dust or other airborne solids.

gases   a vapor that is in a gaseous state

radiation   microwaves, ultraviolet rays, infrared rays, electromagnetic frequencies, ionization, radon

organic   from living sources such as plants

inorganic   from manufactured sources such as solvents

odor   detectable smell from any form of airborne material

Some categories of pollution can contain components from more than one of these areas. Smoke, for example, can consist of solid particles, liquid particulates, and/or gases. Solid particles can also absorb VOCs and other gases, providing an effective delivery system for toxins to the lungs.

ronments was also a major issue. Even as long ago as the late 1800s, some observers reported on the negative effects of such odors in crowded places. One report, from 1898, stated that "two great causes of discomfort, though not the only ones, are excessive temperature and unpleasant odors."

In the 1930s, researchers at Harvard University used controlled experiments to determine how much fresh air was needed to keep people comfortable in an interior environment. Constantin Yaglou and other scientists measured oxygen and carbon dioxide levels, temperature, humidity, and body odor from human subjects, with trained judges used to determine acceptable levels of odor. Their measurements resulted in a set of standards for airflow in building ventilation systems that were used for several decades. In general, they established a relation between temperature, airflow, and the

Ventilation Basics

The ventilation process can be divided into several basic categories:

- movement of outside air to the inside
- filtering/treating the outside air
- mixing outdoor air with indoor air
- distribution of mixed air to building locations
- venting some indoor air to the outside

The recommended minimum amount of air ventilated into an office building is 7.5 liters/second per person [ASHRAE]. This level is set to provide the lowest acceptable amount of carbon dioxide.

Material Effects

Major sources of poor indoor air quality:

- VOCs
- pesticides
- carbon monoxide
- outgassing from building materials
- outgassing from furnishings
- carpet cleaning fluids
- fibers
- fresh paint
- cleaning compounds
- combustion sources
- joint compounds
- formaldehyde
- tobacco smoke
- plasticizers
- carpets
- allergens
- dust
- molds
- caulks
- adhesives

number of occupants in a given amount of space. The higher the temperature and/or the higher the occupancy, the greater the airflow needed to neutralize odors. The minimum standard for outdoor air delivery in buildings has generally been accepted to be 15 cfm (cubic feet per minute) per occupant, a level found to provide an odor level tolerable to 80 percent of occupants.

In recent generations, recommended amounts of outside air for offices have dropped because, it turns out, it takes less replacement air to provide adequate oxygen than it does to remove body odor and, in the modern office environment, most employees have adapted a practice of regular bathing and use of deodorants.

After World War II, it was more common for cigarette smoke to generate odor problems than bodies; ventilation standards for odor removal through the 1980s typically focused on tobacco. With the widespread adoption of smoking bans in commercial buildings, odor in general is a problem mostly associated with chemicals, cleaning fluids, and gases from manmade products.

The population is quickly becoming more sensitive to tobacco smoke as it becomes rarer. One result may be a continuing increase in sensitivities to cigarette smoke and other odors that it may have previously masked. Office environments of the future could require higher and higher degrees of filtering in order to accommodate this new sensitivity.

Another outcome from this pioneering Harvard study was that building occupants have different levels of comfort than visitors. People entering a building for the first time tend to have stronger reactions to odors or other environmental conditions than those working inside.

In the first generation of office ventilation, windows were the only option available. This low-tech solution provided adequate airflow for most operations, but then, like now, was hampered by several negative variables. One was noise, with open windows being a perfect conduit to distractions from outside. Odors and pollution from outside were also unwanted visitors and, in cold weather, uncomfortable outdoor temperatures limited the effectiveness of windows as a source of fresh air.

The availability of electricity provided another option, powered fans. These were quickly adapted for use in rooms and entire buildings to aid airflow, but there were flaws with this technology as well. In some applications, fans provided a more uniform mixing of the air, increasing the efficiency with which odors, unhealthy fumes, and diseases were distributed to building occupants.

Fresh air was long recognized as a key factor in worker effectiveness and health, which helped establish the first guidelines for ventilation. But the concept of the "sick building" is relatively new, surfacing only in the late 1970s. Also referred to as Sick Building Syndrome (SBS) and Office Building Syndrome (OBS), the issue arose in response to the energy crisis in mid-decade, when building owners and managers rushed to reduce the cost of heating, cooling, and lighting structures.

In many cases, an early victim was indoor air quality, which suffered as windows were sealed in order to better control indoor temperatures. One unintended consequence was an extra burden placed on inadequate mechanical ventilation systems, which in many cases were unable to make up for the fresh air previously provided by windows.

Poor ventilation led to increased levels of carbon monoxide, VOCs, and other toxic pollutants, as well as wider infestations of fungus and bacteria — the byproduct of rising levels of humidity — resulting in an increase in the number and severity of health complaints from building tenants. This period also coincided with the introduction of new office technologies, including personal computers, computer printers, copy machines, and fax machines, all of which contributed to rising levels of contaminants in indoor air.

In the boom period of the 1990s, another contributing factor arose: overcrowding. Downsizing, reengineering, and the trend to shuffle more workers into cubicle-laden open spaces added bodies to spaces not designed to handle the load.

Technically speaking, "sick building syndrome" relates to

structures with more than one source of poor indoor air quality linked to health problems. When there is a single known source, the proper term is "building related illness." The latter condition is less common and may involve the contamination of an HVAC system with a single organism, such as Legionnaire's Disease or mold.

But even if a structure has not been diagnosed as "sick," it is more likely than not that the air quality inside poses some risk to the occupants. The Environmental Protection Agency estimates that the pollution level inside the average building is two to five times higher than that outside, a condition generated by recirculating indoor air that picks up contaminants — from the building itself, the furnishings, and its occupants — as well as the unwelcome components lingering from outdoor air and not trapped by filters on the way in. In some U.S. buildings, indoor pollution levels have been measured as 100 times more concentrated than outdoor air.

This condition matters a lot, because average adult Americans spend about 90 percent of their time indoors, and as much as half of this time is likely to be in a work environment. The major source of airborne pollutants is thus indoor air, not the outdoor environment.

Problem Particles

At any given time, both visible and invisible particles may be floating around in an office environment. The general range of size for airborne particles, both liquid and solid, is from 0.005 to 100 microns. This compares to the size of an average human hair, which is 70 microns. In general, inhalable particles are less than 10 microns in diameter.

Dust particles have a direct link to indoor air quality. Dusty air contributes to nasal congestion, sore throats, dizziness, headaches, chest pain, skin irritation, and itchy eyes. For people who are already sensitive to chemical fumes, just about any kind of chemical odor in an office environment is likely to trigger complaints and health problems. These include dizziness, headaches, fatigue, sore throats, a lack of concentration, eye irritation, and other symptoms.

"The results of our review indicate that lower ventilation rates within the normally encountered range were significantly associated with both increased health effects and worsened perceived air quality."

— Seppänne, Fisk, and Mendell
(*Indoor Air 1999*)

One major issue impacting ventilation in office environments is efficiency. When the proper amount of fresh air is provided for interior spaces, energy is required to draw it in from the outside, filter it, heat or cool it, add or remove humidity, and move it around. But in some areas inside buildings, such as bathrooms and kitchens, the rate at which "used" air is removed is higher than elsewhere in the building, a deliberate design to reduce objectionable odors and contaminants. As the air in these specialized areas is removed, it is usually replaced by conditioned air from other areas of the interior, air that has already cost energy — and money. Thus, to provide the appropriate amount of ventilation in these specialized areas, energy and money are wasted.

The appropriate energy-efficient alternative is to provide separate supplies of outside air to any area where the exhaust system increases circulation, reducing the loss of conditioned air from other areas of a building. However, in most cases, existing buildings provide a barrier to making this kind of adaptation, or at require large expenditures and produce major disruptions in the process of adding such supplementary ducting. Another option, also expensive and disruptive, is to add heat-exchangers, mechanical devices which recycle heat from air as it is being exhausted.

Among the newest technologies being utilized to reduce indoor air quality problems, ultraviolet lights are being added to existing HVAC systems and incorporated into new systems.

Sick Buildings

- Estimated percentage of U.S. office buildings with poor indoor air quality: 20–30 percent. [Aerias]

- Estimated annual savings if sick buildings were fixed: $58 billion. [Lawrence Berkeley National Laboratory]

- Estimated annual benefit from improved productivity due to healthy indoor air: $200 billion. [Lawrence Berkeley National Laboratory]

- Estimated financial benefits from improving indoor air quality in offices: 8–17 times more than expenditures. [Lawrence Berkeley National Laboratory]

- Direct medical costs paid by U.S. businesses due to poor indoor air quality: $15 billion per year. [American Journal of Medicine]

- Estimated productivity losses for U.S. businesses due to indoor air quality: 60 million work days per year. [U.S. Environmental Protection Agency]

The UV light is beamed across air flows and neutralizes many common contaminants, including mold spores, bacteria, mildew, and viruses, as well as some solvents. In one test inside three office buildings in Montreal, Canada, the addition of a UV system resulted in a 20 percent decrease in reported symptoms previously linked to indoor air and a 40 percent reduction in respiratory symptoms specifically.

"Designers and managers alike need to understand which aspects of the physical setting promote human performance and productivity. They need to be willing to listen to those who must work in the environments chosen for them by others and to act on the experiences and perceptions these occupants report."
— Stan Aronoff, Audrey Kaplan (*Total Workplace Performance*)

By one estimate, the cost to install a UV system in an existing building with 1,000 occupants is about $50,000, with an additionally annual cost of about $14,000 for maintenance and energy use. This, or other technological improvements to existing HVAC systems, may be an economical investment in the long run. According to research conducted at the Lawrence Berkeley National Laboratory, poor indoor air quality has a significant cost because of lost productivity. Based on national averages, expenditures to improve the quality of indoor air in offices produce benefits 8 to 17 times more than their cost.

In many existing buildings, however, such improvements may be outweighed by continuing building problems due to age, outmoded infrastructure, and deteriorating building materials. Fiberglass lining in ductwork, for example, was commonly used in office construction up through the early 1980s, and is a recurring problem because it releases dangerous particles over time as it deteriorates. If such insulation is used throughout a building's duct system, the cost of replacement can be prohibitive.

The most cost-effective way to reduce energy loss due to HVAC equipment and improve indoor air quality is to add appropriate new equipment to a new design. When it comes to the indoor environment, a build-to-suit project provides the most efficient, effective solution.

The age of buildings is also directly tied to the quality of indoor air. In general, the older the building, the more likely that dust creates a problem during air circulation. Structural defects in older buildings are also associated with a higher level of moisture instrusion, resulting in mold growth. Even some modern buildings can have an elevated risk, often because of ductwork that is lined with fiberglass.

Along with fiberglass particles from insulation elsewhere in a building, the placement in ductwork adds significant problems because as they decay, dangerous airborne particles are distributed along with circulating air. Until recently, some modern construction materials were a common source of formaldehyde and other volatile organic compounds (VOCs) emitted as fumes when newly installed or curing.

"Sick buildings" may generate their own indoor air pollution, but some indoor air problems can also be pulled in from outside sources. Open windows or fresh air ventilation systems, for example, may import car fumes from nearby streets and parking lots or industrial exhaust from neighboring manufacturing facilities.

Human sources of indoor air pollution are particularly troublesome. The main issue here is the inadvertent transmission of diseases, such as the common cold, the flu, and respiratory infections. Viruses are particularly dangerous in closed environments such as offices because they are easily transported by air currents and can be passed on to large numbers of people in a short amount of time.

While viruses and other disease organisms are silent, invisible air pollutants, what causes the most irritation to most office workers are pollutants that can be detected by smell. Odors, even those that are non-harmful, may be strong and generate immediate negative reactions, but in most cases it is less intense smells that produce the most harm.

A lingering sense of discomfort may be the least of reactions; nausea, headaches, or loss of appetite are also linked to low-level objectionable smells. Other than short-term work interruptions due to these kinds of minor health problems, lingering exposure to bad smells can also bump up the level of stress and contribute to absenteeism and employee turnover.

Many kinds of unpleasant odors trigger a negative reaction in humans at extremely low concentrations, even below the threshold of detection of sensitive diagnostic equipment, but the variation in response from person to person is also a complicating factor. What some people notice or object to may not produce the same reaction in others.

On the other hand, the type or source of an odor may be as or more important than its intensity. There are some smells that are considered universally good — the scent from most flowers, for example — while others are considered uniformly bad, even in the smallest concentrations. In many western countries, for instance, body perspiration and its characteristic odor is widely disliked. Even in small amounts, its presence can interfere with the ability of employees to concentrate on their work.

HVAC systems rely on several key technologies to control indoor air quality. Air filters are the most common method, with a wide variety of types available. In many cases, existing HVAC systems can be adjusted to accept higher performance air filters, or altered to add additional levels of filtering. Filters for both ventilation and air conditioning systems are included at the primary point of entry to a building, where the goal is to remove solid particles from the outside air before it is circulated inside.

Secondary filter systems are also common in recirculation, where additional systems are used to distribute air inside of sealed buildings. These filters are critical for the control of pollutants that are produced inside.

"It is generally considered that an important facet of "sick building" syndrome is particulate and gaseous contamination emanating inside the building from occupants, furnishings, building materials, and other sources. One reaction to this has been to revert to the higher outdoor air ventilation rates that were common before the energy crisis. This results in higher energy consumption and a greater concentration of outdoor pollutants."

— George Cunningham
(*Building Design for Human Performance*)

Recirculation systems typically provide an additional level of pollutant control by introducing a steady stream of new filtered air from outside, effectively diluting the level of any contamination that may be present. Recirculation and direct ventilation are also critical for adding oxygen-rich air to environments where human activity is present, because normal respiration removes oxygen and replaces it with carbon dioxide.

With filtering, the more efficient the filter, the more the filter blocks the flow of air. More efficient filtering systems are also more expensive, as they usually require larger fans, motors, and power to run.

One modern innovation for air filters is the electrostatic cleaner. This technology applies a slight electrical charge to the particles in an incoming air stream; the newly-charged particles are attracted to and collected by a plate or surface with the opposite electrical charge. Electrostatic cleaners can be effective at removing even the smallest, microscopic solids, but they are more expensive than traditional systems and cost more to run.

Other technologies sometimes employed to remove contaminants from air are "wet scrubbing" and adsorption. The former involves using water sprays to wash out gaseous elements; the latter employs carbon or other solids to absorb gases and odors.

Poor indoor air quality is, at the least, a common source of complaints by building tenants. Even if no health problems are involved, discomfort and stress are a certain outcome, both directly linked to productivity, job satisfaction, and worker turnover. Also, because an estimated 20–40 percent of the U.S. population has a genetic risk for allergies and asthma, there is always the potential for a small number of workers with these types of health conditions to be threatened by poor air quality in their working environment, a threat that has direct implications for their employers.

Organizations that function with inadequate indoor air quality lose in multiple ways, from paying more for output to a higher cost for healthcare. And because "sick building syndrome" has become a major trend in employee litigation, that may also provide a significant cost in the future.

To date, there has been little activity in the insurance industry with respect to indoor air quality (IAQ)— the notable exceptions being a few highly publicized public health hazards, asbestos was the main example. But there is evidence that this could soon change, adding IAQ to the existing family of issues that affect business insurance rates, because of the growing number of claims related to medical conditions such as respiratory ailments.

The current standard practice for building coverage is to use "pollution exclusions," but the trend is for more states to find such practices invalid. In the last few years, a rising tide of concern about mold in buildings — residential as well as commercial — has spawned a trend in lawsuits and legislation. It may be years before standards are in place to benchmark this critical issue, but paranoia and lawsuit momentum have already made it a factor, and building owners have no choice but to deal with it. As with many other IAQ issues, older buildings are more subject to the conditions that breed and spread mold; the cost of dealing with this problem in existing structures may provide strong support for a build-to-suit alternative.

According to the National Institute for Occupational Safety & Health (NIOSH), as of early 2004, most of the new cases being filed by employees regarding indoor air quality are in non-industrial settings. Among office tenants, 24 percent in a 1988 survey by the Building Owners and Managers

Association reported that poor indoor air quality was a common reason for not renewing a lease (this factor was also related to thermal comfort and the performance of air conditioning systems). In 1999, another survey from this group and the Urban Land Institute reported that indoor air quality was "very important" to 94 percent of businesses surveyed.

"Increasing productivity involves more than just downsizing space and staffing. If cost cutting produces an uncomfortable, poorly planned and inefficient work environment, the amount of money saved may be outweighed by the negative impact on employee productivity, including low morale, increased absenteeism, lack of creativity, more errors and poor internal communication."

— ASID ("The Impact of Interior Design on the Bottom Line")

EXECUTIVE SUMMARY
Indoor Air Quality and Health

Some aspects of the indoor environment in offices provoke more than grumbling, they produce sickness. Sickness in the workforce is a significant issue because it adds to the cost of doing business. Workers that are not healthy do not work up to capacity and those that are absent because of illness produce no work at all, even while being paid.

Indoor Air Quality is increasingly implicated in the rate of illness in offices, and much of this impact is directly related to the age and inefficiency of buildings and HVAC systems. Retrofits and maintenance are practical tactics in some cases, but the expense and disruptions that accompany major HVAC alterations may outweigh their benefits.

In the short term, pushing more air through existing ventilation systems may keep some problems at bay. Long term, however, the only effective solution is starting from scratch with well-designed new structures that can take advantage of the latest technology.

Office Noise

"Clearly, the physical setting has a direct effect on individual task performance and the work process as a whole. If the work environment hinders the successful completion of tasks — disruptive noise when a worker is trying to concentrate, for one — one might expect either a lower level of performance or a less effective performance (that is, it takes longer)."

— Jean Wineman (*Behavioral Issues in Office Design*)

Noise can be painful, even harmful. Continued exposure to extreme levels of noise — explosions, gunfire, industrial machinery, amplified music, etc. — leads to an eventual loss of hearing and, potentially, deafness. Across all industries, noise induced hearing loss is the number one among all occupational diseases. In most office environments, however, the problem with noise is not pain or loss of hearing, but a distraction that has a negative effect on productivity and job satisfaction.

Office noise varies in sound level, characteristics, and continuity, and office workers vary in their reaction to it. Some people thrive in noisy environments, others in total silence. In between is a range where most employees function at least adequately, with a background sound level generated by conversations of others in a room, sounds transmitted through office walls, ceilings, and windows, and the hum of ventilation systems, copiers, computer printers, and other equipment.

The sounds of an office environment are made even more complex because not every sound creates the same reaction to everyone exposed to it. By definition, a sound is considered noise only when it is unwelcome. It does not necessary have to be loud, just intrusive. In practice, this means that a phone conversation is noise if it intrudes on the working zone of another person even though it is a necessary part of the working zone of the person participating in it.

Much more than with light or temperature, sound in an office environment presents a complex and difficult factor to identify, much less remedy. Adding to the complexity, too little noise — although rare compared to the opposite extreme — also provokes complaints from some office workers. In these kinds of situations, the absence of "normal" office sounds produces an uneasy feeling and tenants can find it difficult to maintain their regular activities.

"Without doubt, noise as a typical stressor has a negative impact not only on speech intelligibility, performance, and well-being at work, but also on regeneration possibilities after work."

— *Helmut Strasser, Kristina Gruen, Werner Koch (Occupational Ergonomics, 1999/2000)*

In fact, some studies have reported a correlation between rising levels of noise and easier communications. That is, some employees find it easier to talk to others when there is a higher level of background noise, perhaps because it provides a convenient masking effect. When others around you are busy talking among themselves, it is less likely that they will be paying attention to what you are saying in your own conversations.

But while communications may be a key component of

Sound Health

Negative effects from exposure to loud or sudden noises include:

- high blood pressure
- muscle tension
- fatigue

- slowed rate of breathing
- general stress
- depression

teamwork, enhancing the effects of people working in groups, the noise that it generates can also cause problems for those individuals trying to concentrate on individual tasks, also an important function within organizations. Conversational noise also is prone to the "restaurant effect," in which individuals in a room react to rising noise levels by increasing the intensity of their speech. The result is an upward spiral of noise which can quickly lead to uncomfortable levels.

Unlike construction sites or heavy metal concerts, noise in the office environment is not simply a matter of loudness. In some surveys, for example, office tenants cite human conversation as generating more intrusive noise than ringing telephones. This is because in this environment, conversations are often clear enough to be understood, providing a more complex type of sound — conveying more content and meaning — than a simple ring tone.

Part of the listener's brain latches onto words and phrases, producing a level of distraction not easily ignored. And this occurs even though the typical sound level of a human conversation is only half as loud as a telephone ring. Research has shown that in a standard open room, the content of a human conversation can be understood by someone standing more than 30 feet away.

Sound Standards

Ideally, office structures are designed to limit the amount of unwanted noise and to control reverberations, or unwanted side-effects of noise.

Recommended sound levels:

- open office areas   40 dB
- private offices   30 dB
- conference rooms   30 dB

Typical sound level generated by one person speaking to another at a distance of 3 feet: 60 dB

In office environments, sound factors consist of:

- privacy, the need to conduct communications without being overheard
- concentration, the need to perform activities without being distracted
- communications, the need to insure understanding without confusion because of distortion or conflicting sound sources

In laboratory settings, sound levels can be measured and human reactions to them studied. Among the health effects of exposure to loud or sudden noises are high blood pressure, slowed rate of breathing, tension, general stress, fatigue, and depression. When people are continually exposed to noise, the general response is acclimatization. Not all people acclimatize at the same rate or with similar results, however, and acclimatization doesn't necessarily mean the noise is no longer a problem. Rather, it recedes as a major source of interruption and becomes more of a background irritant. In either case, it has a negative effect on concentration, mental energy, and productivity.

Individual response to noise can vary from day to day and even during the same day, in response to mood, psychological situations related to families, and other personalized factors. Some studies have shown that individuals who grew up in large families are generally more tolerant of noise than those who come from smaller families.

Acoustics and noise control in offices are considered very important issues by 90 percent of office tenants, and 81 percent of office workers believe their productivity would improve if their offices were less noisy.

A similar connection comes from cultural backgrounds; individuals who grew up in noisy urban environments are generally more tolerant of noise than those who were raised in quieter neighborhoods. Another compounding factor is that individuals may complain about noise selectively, finding it less tolerable if coming from activities or people they dislike.

Despite this variation, noise is considered a problem by the majority of office workers. A recent study from the American Society of Interior Designers (ASID) reported that noise reduction was a major concern; 81 percent of office workers surveyed believed their productivity would increase in response to less noisy conditions in their offices. In a national survey of office tenants conducted by BOMA (Building Owners and Managers Association) and the Urban Land Institute, acoustics and noise control was rated "very important" by 90 percent of the respondents.

Speech Privacy

In open plan offices, it would be extremely expensive to provide complete acoustic privacy to each occupant, assuming it was even technically possible. Because the main component of noise in open offices is human conversation, the more realistic goal is to provide speech privacy, reducing the background chatter so that its intelligibility level is low and therefore less likely to provide the recognizable content that constitutes disruption.

Articulation index (AI)		0.00–1.00

A rating of 0 means that a conversation is completely unintelligible; 1 denotes complete understanding.

0.05 or less	confidential privacy	speech heard but not understood
0.05–0.15	normal speech privacy	speech heard but requires effort to understand

In some surveys, employees report the number one factor related to doing a good job is the ability to concentrate without interference from noise or other distractions. But it is not just noise itself that is the problem. In general, the degree that noise becomes an interference is related to its predictability — unpredictable, intermittent sounds are more disagreeable than those that are constant or regular — as well as its intensity and frequency.

In one experiment, two groups of workers were exposed to the same level of noise. One group was equipped with controls that could deaden this sound, but were asked not to do so.

The results showed that the group with the noise control outperformed the group without this ability. As with similar studies measuring reactions to comfort zones, it is the availability of the control — not the control itself — that has a positive result. In office environments, the suggestion is that noise in itself is less damaging than the lack of control over it. It is disruptive because it is out of a person's control.

Even though noise in the office workplace is mostly an annoyance, not a major known cause of health problems, it can have the same effect. If noise is identified as a reason that work is unsatisfactory, employees may choose another option, calling in sick. Excessive noise can also contribute to employee turnover and is likely to have a negative effect on recruiting and hiring new workers.

In office environments, noise has been implicated in:
- an increase in errors
- difficulty with communications
- memory and recall lapses
- difficulty in learning and comprehension

Many different studies have attempted to measure human responses to noise and determine a range of negative reaction. The results, however, do not conclusively point to a danger, merely a link between certain kinds of sound and the response.

In general:
- when people are more satisfied with their jobs or lives, they are more likely to tolerate higher levels of noise
- activities requiring more mental activity and concentration are more likely to be negatively impacted by noise

Office Noises

Noises reported as being "most bothersome" in office environments:

- ringing telephones
- human conversations face-to-face
- human conversations on the telephone
- ventilation systems

Noises reported as being "least bothersome" in office environments:

- background music
- outside sounds
- office equipment

Suspended ceilings are a typical structure element in many offices. This functional design permits easy access to overhead lighting and in many applications, overhead distribution computers and telecommunications network wiring. Suspended ceilings are also designed with acoustic properties that initially benefit open office layouts. The individual tiles in these structures are sound absorbent, helping dampen and limit the transmission of background noise from one part of a room to another.

This original benefit, however, is limited in effectiveness when larger rooms are subdivided with partitions. Often, walls added in these situations only extend from the floor to the suspended ceiling, leaving a gap above the tiles through which sounds travel from enclosure to enclosure.

Acoustic Standards Rules of Thumb

- recommended height of room dividers 65 inches

- Sound Transmission Class (STC) rating
  for sound blocking 20 or higher

- Noise Reduction Coefficient (NRC)
  rating for panels .60

- Speech Frequency Sound Absorption
  rating for panels 80

- Articulation class (AC) rating
  for ceilings 180–200

- Sound masking system level NC 40

- Noise Reduction Coefficient (NRC)
  rating for carpeting .20 or higher

- Impact insulation class (IIC) rating
  for flooring 60 or higher

- NRC for ceilings 0.75 or higher

In some older buildings, vibration may also be a widespread problem. Depending on the building materials and designs used, footsteps, door closings and openings, and other actions generate vibrations that are carried throughout a floor or from one floor to another. Depending on the material, wall and ceiling surfaces can also be the source of another sound problem, reflection.

In some kinds of existing buildings, remodeling can provide effective relief for some kinds of noise. Sound absorbent materials, for example, such as carpeting, ceiling tiles, and wall coverings, can be added to reduce vibrations and reflections. The cost of the material, however, is not the only expense associated with this kind of remedial action. Labor costs for retrofits are often higher than for new construction because of difficulty fitting around obstacles and fixtures in use and such work typically requires temporary relocation of employees, a major cost.

The majority of contemporary offices now include at least some open areas divided into cubicles, an attempt to provide some acoustic protection for their occupants. In fact, one of the reasons that cubicles were developed (in the 1960s) was to reduce the level of noise and other distractions without requiring the expense and floor space required by traditional enclosed offices.

Acoustic Influences

Almost every physical element of an office structure can affect the acoustics of a room. All of them are linked in a complex interactive pattern that involves sound reflection, absorption, diffraction, and blocking.

- floor dimensions
- ceiling height
- floor covering
- wall covering
- window dimensions
- window placement
- number of windows
- number of doors
- type and placement of lighting fixtures

In open office settings, there are typically more complaints about noise than in other settings. This is not surprising, as this layout style places more people together in one space with minimal barriers to the transmission of normal office sounds, especially conversations.

It is not possible for any cubicle design to completely isolate its space from the sounds of the room it is in. As long as there is a physical gap or opening, some sound from outside will be transmitted. Because sound waves radiate directly out from their source, cubicle walls will block those waves that it intercepts. Reflected sounds from ceilings and walls are what gets through. But even low cubicle walls are effective at reducing sound levels, and the higher the walls, the greater the effect.

Engineering tactics used in cubicle design to reduce the effects of incoming sound waves include careful placement of panels to redirect waves away from occupants and the addition of baffles, storage units, or other wall modification to do the same. These units are effective as reflectors, but they can also reduce the effectiveness of panels that are already designed to absorb sound with soft, textured surfaces.

Where the occupant sits can also be a major factor. For example, the closer the occupant sits to a cubicle wall, the less reflected noise will be a problem because the center of such a space often concentrates sound waves reflected off the vertical panels.

Yet even with the best placement, design, and materials, cubicles may still provide a distracting environment for some users. To achieve the highest level of noise control, researchers are continually improving the tools for this job. One focus of this effort is new materials for cubicle walls, engineered to absorb more sound, especially that transmitted from one neighboring unit to another.

Stress

Stress has a constant presence in the modern office. It comes from pressure to improve productivity, to perform more work with fewer people, and to compete for limited positions, as well as from the complicated affects of personal and professional lives.

All things considered, the physical office environment is most always a secondary contributor to stress. But if stress is already present, secondary triggers from the environment are more likely to push it out of control. Office noise, over-crowded spaces, and poor indoor air quality, among many such factors, are more than enough to escalate stress to unhealthy levels.

People pushed beyond their manageable stress levels perform below standard work, miss deadlines, generate more errors, and are more accident prone. Stress also produces fatigue and lowers resistance to disease, leading to higher rates of absenteeism and employee turnover.

Stress produces some obvious signs — headaches, irritability, stomach upsets, sleep disorders, nervousness, depression, physical and mental fatigue — as well as unwanted internal changes — elevated blood pressure, hypertension, increased levels of adrenaline and cortisol, peptic ulcers, and increased levels of blood sugars. Over time, chronic stress conditions are linked to serious health problems, increasing the risk of or magnifying the effects of coronary heart disease and arteriosclerosis, among others.

The competitive atmosphere of work may not provide much relief for the primary causes of stress, but physical office environments are a prime target for reducing and eliminating its secondary causes.

This is of increasing interest as cubicle sizes shrink; the shorter the distance from one cubicle to another, the more energy left for sound waves to create a distraction. In older cubicle designs, noise control was attempted through absorption, but when short distances are involved, absorption is relatively ineffective. The latest methods instead rely on sound blocking, using heavy, dense materials that eliminate the transmission of sound waves.

Another method has also proven useful at reducing the distraction from background noises in open offices. Sophisticated sound masking systems generate a type of "white noise" that

Tomorrow's Noise

Noise is expected to become more of an issue in the future because of distinct trends underway in the office environment. These include:

- fewer enclosed offices, more open floor plans
- higher density of workers in the same space
- lower cubicle partitions
- increasing use of speaker phones, cell phones, and phone headsets, adding to the amount of phone conversations contributing to background noise throughout a given space
- increasing use of desktop videoconferencing, adding a new source of voice conversations
- increasing use of digital voice transcriptions and voice-controlled software
- more dedicated team areas with an increase in collaboration and personal communications

counteracts the hum of human conversation by making it unintelligible and therefore less intrusive.

In practice, it may require all of the above applications to control office noise because an incorrect balance can simply turn one kind of acoustic problem into another. The effort to re-engineer a noisy office can turn into an ongoing, expensive proposition with no permanent solution. As with other nagging barriers in existing office space, the most effective long-term solution may be to develop a build-to-suit environment that is designed right to begin with.

The use of office space can be altered to alleviate some noise problems. A group or activity that generates more noise, for example, can be placed in a location where the noise is less likely to generate complaints or be a problem. Segregation can also be accompanied by selective retrofitting to isolate a group or activity.

Individuals with specific noise complaints may also be targeted to deal with the issue. In this case, insulation or placement is applied to reduce the problem coming in from the surrounding area.

Office procedures have also been implemented to deal with some kinds of noise. Policies and training can be employed to help sensitize the issue of loud conversations, disruptive behavior, and appropriate use of spaces. Some organizations also use designated spaces for both extremes, quiet zones for concentration and meeting areas for conversation exchanges.

Office organization can also help relieve some problems. Public address systems, for example, may be a key source of unwanted disruptions. The solution may be pagers, telephone paging, or other technology-driven alternatives. Job activities that require a lot of telephone interaction may be shifted to sites where such conversations do not interfere with job activities that require individual concentration.

What is to gain by reducing noise in office settings? A research project (Armstrong World Industries/Dynasound) reported an average improvement in effectiveness of 13 percent by office workers in an environment where noise from equipment, mechanical systems, and conversations was reduced.

"A series of studies conducted over the past 12 years has convincingly documented that conversational distraction and uncontrolled noise is the primary cause of productivity loss within offices."

— ASID ("Sound Solutions")

EXECUTIVE SUMMARY
Office Noise

Noise represents one of the biggest barriers to effective work practices in modern offices. Although some office equipment may be getting quieter, there is also an increasing amount of it in the average office, adding to the existing environment of meetings, casual conversations, and phone calls.

The current trend to place more office workers in open plan layouts adds additional weight to this problem, which is fundamentally linked to the design of interior space and the material used in its construction. Existing office spaces can be made quieter with the careful placement of partitions and added insulation, but these alterations only provide partial solutions.

New office space can be specifically designed with the right acoustics for the intended use, segregating necessarily noisy activities from those that require isolation.

Office Size and Layout

"A building is a visible, concrete manifestation of a social group or social institution. And since every social institution has smaller groups and institutions within it, a human building will always reveal itself, not as a monolith, but as a complex of these smaller institutions, made manifest and concrete too."

— Christopher Alexander *(A Pattern Language)*

Contemporary office activity is constantly evolving. In previous business eras, this was less evident. Then, large groups of employees could expect their working tasks to remain static for most, if not all, of their careers. These days, however, change is the norm, not only over a career but often from week to week.

In a typical work week in the average office today, many employees shift from solitary desk work — often involved with repetitive data entry or other computer drudgery — to small meetings to training sessions, often in different parts of the same building, punctuated by irregular trips to copy machines, fax machines, file cabinets, managers' offices, and other scattered destinations.

Regular desk work, too, can often vary. Typical desk activities include reading and editing paper documents, typing and entering data into computer systems, Web searches, reading and writing email, retrieving and filing paper documents, and participating in online discussions or interactive work sessions.

In an earlier era, any time away from a desk might have been seen as a valuable break in a tedious routine. However, offices, in their first few phases of existence, were seen more as an extension of the factory floor than a form of knowledge work and time away from the desk was a negative factor for productivity.

These days, the routine involved with computers and workstations also includes more movement away from the desktop, not because there are more scheduled breaks but because of the nature of the modern office. Work often includes frequent interactions with other employees that require mobility.

In general, as more organizations incorporate an element of team work activities into their standard business processes, more employees spend more time away from their desks. A recent Workplace Index Survey (Steelcase/Opinion Research Corporation) reported that only one half of a typical work week was spent at desks. Further, 42 percent of survey respondents reported they spent the majority of their time standing, not sitting. The average amount of time per week spent at meetings (away from desks): 7 hours.

> *"Our research ... suggests that more open office environments, like team-oriented bullpens and workstation pods, significantly benefit communication that speeds the overall work process while contributing to high-quality work and employee satisfaction with their job."*
>
> — Franklin Becker and William Sims
> (*Offices That Work*)

Too often, however, the nature of movement within a structure is disruptive rather than supportive. The majority of office layouts predate the needs of the businesses that inhabit them. Individuals or groups that have frequent interaction with other people — as well as shared resources such as copy

Space Glossary

- **circulation ratio**. A figure representing the relative amount of space used for movement within a building compared to the square footage used for workspace. This includes hallways, aisles, and transition areas. As a rule of thumb, this figure is typically 20–30 percent.

- **employees housed/occupancy**. The total number of people working in a building, including both full time equivalents (FTEs) and part time workers.

- **enclosed to open ratio**. A figure representing the number of employees in private rooms compared to those working in open area (including cubicles). Some types of businesses — such as law firms, or consultants — traditionally utilize more private rooms than others — call centers, insurance offices, and data processing centers.

- **gross density ratio**. A figure representing the square footage of usable space per employee. Ultimately not a very useful measurement, as this figure includes shared space and support space, such as hallways, storage, meeting rooms, etc. Also the figure will vary considerably depending on the ratio of cubicle space to private rooms. In the early part of the 21st century in the U.S., this figure ranges from 175 to 325 square feet per person.

- **meeting room ratio**. A figure representing the number of employees per meeting room. In general, offices with a higher number of private rooms have less dependence on dedicated meeting rooms than offices with more open or shared space. The size of meeting rooms — small rooms for teams or lecture machines, fax equipment, etc. — may waste time because of the distances they have to travel.

Movement inside offices is also a source of distraction, especially when passageways are routed through open work areas where cubicle dividers do not adequately screen occupants from this traffic. Along with the wasted time it takes to move from one area to another, disruption takes a toll on output, reducing the quality and amount of production.

Proximity is the key factor in determining how offices are laid out. When two departments or areas have lots of interaction, it makes sense to put them close together in order to reduce the amount of time it takes to get from one to another. Similarly, links between assignments and shared equipment — fax machines, copiers, etc. — suggest shorter distances, but access should also be a factor of frequency of use. Personnel who make heavy use of fax equipment need closer proximity than those with sporadic use.

---

rooms for large groups — will impact this ratio, as will the frequency of meetings — the more meetings, the greater the need for multiple rooms to reduce conflicts in scheduling. Typical range for this factor: 1–10 to 1–100.

- **rentable square footage**. A figure that represents the realistic use of leased space in a shared building. This includes entry areas, public corridors, rest rooms, and other areas where tenants or visitors cross paths.

- **total square footage**. A figure determined by the overall dimensions of the inside floor space of a building.

Office layouts should be designed to improve productivity, worker satisfaction, and communication. All of these factors are instrumental in the health of an organization, but economics is also an overriding issue. Most business are located in leased space that was designed for other uses or, just as inappropriately, designed generically for the widest range of uses, limiting the efficiency needed for a specific business application.

Average Space

The general trend for office staffs is less space per person. As of 2003, it was 347 square feet, down about 2 percent a year. Over a recent five year period, offices for upper management have experienced the most shrinkage, down 15 percent, from 280 to 239 square feet, and space for senior management personnel shrank 12 percent, from 193 to 169 square feet. [IFMA]

In terms of usable space (workspace plus associated storage and special space) per person, the average in the private sector is about 250 square feet. The U.S. Government estimates its office employees have about 200 square feet per person.

In the five years between 1997 and 2002, the amount of space dedicated to private offices has also decreased, down 3 percent, while open space plans have gathered momentum, increasing space use by 3 percent.

Cubicle size is shrinking along with general floor space. In some applications, cubicles now average about 8 square feet per person, down from 12 square feet a decade earlier.

There may be too much space dedicated to private offices, or not enough. Unlike open spaces used for bullpens or cubicles, private offices represent the most inflexible use of building space because their walls, wiring, and HVAC connections were designed to be permanent or defy speed or cost-effective alterations. Also, the size of individual enclosed rooms may not be suitable for present-day uses. Large rooms may be too big for cost-effective use by a single person; small rooms can be inadequate for the desk space, files, and other fixtures needed for a specific user.

Open space in older buildings presents another set of problems. The size of open spaces in these structures was typically tied to the engineering involved. The number and placement of walls or columns was determined by the construction materials and format, not the use of the space. Thus, an open area otherwise suitable for a group of cubicles could be too small to hold all the cubicles needed to house a work group or department, forcing a unified business element to be split.

Or, the open space might be too large, leading to an inappropriate mix of business elements. Occupants from one set of cubicles, for example, might need semi-privacy to handle confidential phone calls but be mislocated by the limitations of space, stuck next to a set of cubicles where the occupants need a distraction-free environment to perform calculations at workstations.

Organizations often go to great lengths to modify their existing space. This effort may come from a realization that the space is a barrier to effectiveness or because the nature of the business activity changes, requiring different use of the space. In either case, older buildings can become budgetary black holes, sucking up funds for materials and labor but never providing full satisfaction.

Categories of Space

- **corridor**. As a rule of thumb, 20–25 percent of the usable floor space (all offices, open rooms, shared facilities, meeting rooms, etc.) is dedicated to corridors for movement, with widths ranging from 6 feet (public hallways) to 3 feet (space between desks).

- **cubicle**. A semi-enclosed workspace arranged in rows or other groupings. Enclosures are created by partitions of varying heights, from 4 feet high to 6 feet high or slightly higher. Modular fixtures allow for a range of sizes and configurations. Typical sizes: 6x6 feet, 8x6 feet, 8x10 feet, 9x12 feet (36–108 square feet).

- **executive office**. A private office with room for several desks, credenzas, and often a conference table. Size typically varies according to the size of an organization: 15x15 feet up 20x15 feet or larger (225–300 square feet).

- **manager's office**. A private office with room for a desk, file storage, bookshelf, and often seating for several people. Typical size: 10x15 feet or slightly smaller (150 square feet or less).

- **meeting room**. Modern offices generally rely on smaller meeting rooms, with seating for 20–30 participants. Planning considerations include access to and use of communications and the Internet, audiovisual/projection capability, whiteboards, acoustic barriers to isolate group activities, and flexible seating. Increasing use of laptops, PDAs, and teleconferencing and videoconferencing also requires consideration for these kinds of technologies to be used. Rooms that accommodate larger numbers may require special acoustical treatments, audio systems, and theater seating for line of sight. Also, when meeting rooms are to be used frequently, rest room facilities in close proximity are a practical addition. Typically, sizes accommodate 15–35 square feet per person, depending on the type of seating arrangement.

- **open plan office.** An open room large enough to contain multiple cubicles or other shared workspaces, such as pods (4–6 workstations segregated by a partition) or bullpens (4–12 desks grouped together).

- **shared facility.** Individual workers or divisions may share access to equipment or fixtures that are placed in rooms or areas where they can be easily accessed. This includes photocopiers, fax machines, shredders, network printers, paper files, reference material, coffee or vending machines, microwaves and refrigerators, dining tables, and others.

- **shared office.** Enclosed office used by two or more occupants.

- **special purpose room.** An enclosed space adapted for a specialized activity. These rooms include laboratories, testing facilities, archival storage, mainframe computing, libraries, communications centers, recording studios, exhibit halls, demonstration or sales rooms, and others.

- **training facility.** Modern training formats may require space different than that for meetings, because of dependency on the Internet, digital multimedia, individual workstations, and videoconferencing.

- **workstations.** Workstations are individual computer monitors and keyboards connected to local area networks or the Internet, often placed in rows or groups in open areas.

> *"The performance of an individual knowledge worker tends to be highly dependent on his or her interaction with coworkers. While the measurement of individual performance may be desirable for certain types of research, such as the effects of the work setting on the individual, in terms of the organization's objectives, it is generally more useful and valid to measure the productivity of groups of knowledge workers rather than the productivity of individuals."*
>
> — Stan Aronoff and Audrey Kaplan (*Total Workplace Performance*)

The problems range from the added cost of construction work underway amid ongoing business activities to the inadequacy of stop-gap measures. The former represents the element of disruption of regular routines — noise, construction traffic, new sources of pollution — and the latter, the reality that a remodeling fix is only a partial solution. For example, adding full partitions to a room with a suspended ceiling rarely creates new acoustically-private enclosures because the new partitions cannot block sound transmissions in the air space created by the ceiling itself.

Even when existing space is adequate for existing uses, the uses themselves are often prone to change. A reality of the modern business climate is that job tasks and responsibilities are constantly evolving, producing new demands on organization structures and, often, structures themselves. Work groups, for example, may be created overnight for projects or reorganized to improve productivity. The number of individual workers in a group flexes along with the existence of the groups themselves, altering the physical location of workspaces, how many people work within a defined space, and the proximity of one group to another.

In order for workspace to accommodate this reality, it must be flexible. Flexibility in layouts includes the ability to add or subtract single work spaces quickly and affordably, the placement of a group in a new location, and the portability of shared office features that support individuals and groups.

In older buildings, merely adding employees or packing more workers into an existing space outpaces the ability of HVAC or lighting systems to provide the minimum standards of support. Communications, too, presents a barrier to effective flexibility in layouts.

Individual employees these days typically need links to the local computer network (LAN), central phone system, and Internet, components of an office system that can be tedious and expensive to reroute or rewire. Even if a remodeling project adds the latest wiring systems to provide greater flexibility with a given set of networking needs, this wiring system can easily become obsolete in the rapidly-changing world of digital communications technology. Without a built-in capability for adding such wiring — missing in most older structures — the whole task may have to be repeated in the future.

One barrier to improved productivity in some offices is just this kind of communications limitation. Faced with the expense and disruption of new wiring, some organizations continue using outmoded formats, or, worse, select a new system based on the limitations of the building, not the effectiveness of the technology itself.

Growth presents yet another barrier to effective use of office

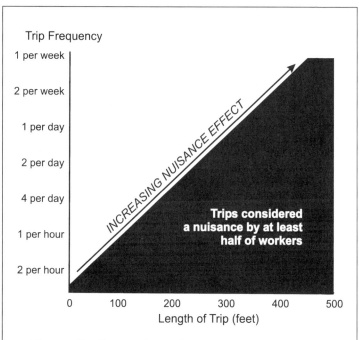

Almost all office work involves some movement, but if the trips are too frequent or too far, they not only waste time, they are part of general dissatisfaction with the office environment, a condition that affects job satisfaction, absenteeism, and turnover. The graph above [adapted from Alexander, *A Pattern Language*, 1977] illustrates the results of a survey of office employees, with a direct relationship between their movement inside an office and how much aggravation such trips may cause. According to Christopher Alexander, the survey author, "If two parts of an office are too far apart, people will not move between them as often as they need to; and if they are more than one floor apart, there will be almost no communication between the two."

space. In many situations, organizations limit the amount of space they lease based on their current needs. If growth occurs during the span of a lease, there may be little choice but to cram more people into existing space. In some cases, this means decreasing the size of cubicles in open areas or adding modified cubicles in corridors or space that was previously used for breaks or meetings.

The justification may be financial — the cost of breaking a lease to move to a large space — and the gain obvious — more employees working in a given space, reducing the cost of overhead per worker. But the implications for long-term growth are not so rosy. When too many people are packed into a space not designed to handle the load, everything from individual health to productivity suffers.

"The design of the physical aspects of the workplace can create certain psychological conditions, e.g., feelings of privacy or crowding and of status and importance, or the converse — perceptions of anonymity and unimportance."

— Jan Noyes (*Designing for Humans*)

One of the most visible elements of office layouts is a traditional reflection of rank and status. Those with higher levels of authority have the most space. This rule is further subdivided by another visible element of office culture: private offices distinguish rank from the masses. Even in open spaces with acreage divided by rows and rows of cubicles, most organizations rely on cubicle size to distinguish between hierarchies of job functions, with the largest cubicles going to those with the most authority.

This is not an artificial set of rules forced on the millions of

Activity and Office Space

breaks

Vending machines, cafeterias, facilities for microwaves and refrigerators, seating/tables designed for casual dining. This reduces the need for staff to leave the premises for lunch or other food quests.

bullpen/pod

Space large enough to hold groups of desks with minimal partitions between each. Bullpens provide a practical use of space resources for work activities performed by groups. Pods are similar, but are based on groups of workstations segregated by a partition.

casual conversation

Meeting areas such as break rooms, lounges, or comfortable seating near water fountains and windows that permit unscheduled person-to-person communications, important for creativity and the exchange of information.

concentration

Private offices, "caves," or other enclosures that can be used for temporary periods of high-concentration work (no distractions, heavily insulated for noise, doors or other barriers to limit drop-in traffic).

cubicles

Partitioned enclosures used for various types of work activities.

entry/reception

Areas for receiving clients or guests.

flex-use

Also referred to as hoteling, moteling, or free address. Accommodations designed for employees who spend a lot of time off premises and do not need a permanent cubicle or office. Fulltime space represents a waste of resources; parttime space can create "turf wars" over any workspace that is available.

private office
The right number and size of rooms to meet the needs of a staff.

open-office plan
Any size room large enough to be practically divided into cubicles, each having from two to four panels or screens high enough to shield occupants while sitting. Such formats allow cubicle sizes to be changed to meet demands and occupants are able to be shifted without much disruption.

parking
Parking areas that are close to work areas can be considered an important and practical necessity. Need is often associated with the severity of the weather, frequency of trips away from the office during the day, and hours worked after dark. Safety and protection from the elements are the underlying motivations.

team meeting
Small conference rooms or casual seating in open areas close to workspaces.

shared facilities
Easy access to restrooms, water, break rooms, shared equipment (fax, copiers, computer printers, etc.), and any other specialized features of a business.

people who work in offices, but a reflection of the reality that is also mirrored in the size of homes, the relative luxuries of automobiles, and even the quality of clothing people wear. In recent years, however, the drive to improve productivity and competitiveness has led many company presidents and office designers to rethink how — and if — status should be represented in the workplace.

By and large, the majority of office workers do not report dissatisfaction with hierarchies of authority in the workplace. It is not the purpose of bosses or the perks they may have that is a problem; in fact, clear lines of authority and divisions of power can enhance performance in an organization.

The office, as a second home, is divided into public and private territory. A workspace, either a private or a cubicle, can enhance job satisfaction because it provides a safe haven, a comfortable environment for work activities, and a separation necessary to create a zone of concentration.

Space Assignment Standards

How are office work spaces allocated?

status/job title	27 percent
task needs	18 percent
equality (same space for everyone)	14 percent
team requirements	14 percent
space available basis	7 percent
[Steelcase Workplace Index]	

When the first cubicles began to be installed in offices in the 1960s, in fact, one of the prime motivations was to eliminate one of the observed shortcomings of the prevailing office environment of the time, a lack of personal space. Before the cubicle era dawned, personal space in offices was defined by desktops and drawers, not enough definition to develop a sense of belonging.

This sense of privacy may not require an enclosed space, lockable door, or other means of protection. But a private office may be necessary for many kinds of business activity because of the privacy it provides.

Some businesses that adopted open office plans over the past few decades have discovered they can be a nuisance and even a threat to organizational structure. Too many companies rushed to adopt this form of layout just because it was "trendy" or offered a compelling economic advantage. For those who did take special care to involve employees in the decision, or pushed the move on workers whose activities were negatively impacted by the open nature of the cubicle, failure was a common result. In some cases, open office layouts have been abandoned — or as least modified — and private offices reinstituted in order to return stability to staffs.

Some of the mistakes made with the open office system involved inappropriate assignments that appeared to be reductions in rank. That is, higher ranking workers suddenly found themselves in cubicles, no longer distinguished by office size even if true rank and compensation remained the same. In a few reported cases, these moves were made even more galling when some executives or managers had the opposite assignment, to office suites, wings, or floors completely isolated from the new open office space.

Management consultants may differ on how useful cubicles can be, but they do caution companies against making radical changes to an existing office structure without careful planning and full disclosure to employees in advance. Plus, these moves are thought to be most successful if they are part of wider, permanent changes in business practices that are system-wide, avoiding the appearance of unequal treatment.

Other indications also indicate that open office formats are not for everybody. A careful study of what kind of business activity is performed is crucial to determining what the most appropriate use of space should be. The types of communications needed are a key factor. If there is a lot of personal conversations that involve proprietary or privileged information — as in a legal firm, for instance — neither the employees or the clients would be well served if the conversations could be overheard.

> "Workspace design needs to facilitate interaction. On the other hand, good design must also provide an appropriate level of audio and visual privacy."
>
> — Janice Linster
> (project director, Ellerbe Beckett, Inc.)

Privacy is one significant issue when determining the best use of space, concentration is another. The workspace has to complement the activity taking place in it and activities that require single-minded focus — programming, copy writing, decision making, for example — are best served by spaces solidly segregated from other employees.

Despite any well-reasoned logic about equality and fairness in office culture, some employees — perhaps most — would likely choose a private office over a cubicle if given the choice. Some studies, in fact, have demonstrated a major impact on

Privacy

In office environments, privacy is a subjective concept. A private office may provide more privacy than a cubicle, but it is only as private as the occupant and office activity permit. On the other hand, bullpens or other shared workspace provide much less privacy than a private office, but occupants here can develop a consistant personal space and a sense of privacy by establishing and heeding rules for distractive behavior.

In general, studies show that the amount of privacy varies as much by type of space as by the degree of control an occupant has over the space and intrusions from outside. To some degree, a clear sense of territory is as important or more so than an effective visual or acoustic barrier. Elements that produce a strong territorial message also can enhance an occupant's sense of private space, and a sense of privacy to go with it.

Another general rule of office privacy: the more routine the work, the more likely that interactions are not harmful, and in fact, help prevent stress and boredom rather than decrease work effectiveness.

In work requiring teams and groups, participants generally accept less privacy as a trade-off for improved communications and other necessary interactions.

In work requiring concentrated individual effort or confidential communications, participants generally prefer isolation — visual and acoustic.

The most functional office layouts permit a mix of both interactive and isolated workspace. Here, the goal is the ability of participants to move from one type of activity to another and match the space to the activity, either allowing or restricting interaction as needed.

selection of employment based on the type of workspace that comes with the job. Workers dissatisfied with an assignment to a cubicle may transfer to another division — or even quit to take another job — in order to acquire this coveted environment. And in a healthy economy with an increasing number of jobs, applicants may be more likely to select their employers based on this kind of office assignment, all other factors being equal. A private office has clout, and in determining the layout of office buildings, companies and facility managers should not underrate this potential.

On the other hand, some kinds of work are enhanced by interactions between workers. The growing popularity of teams in business is not just because many organizations are following a trend; team activity has a synergistic effect, allowing a group of people to accomplish more together than if they were working independently.

But if teams are part of the work picture and the work environment does not support them, output suffers. In open office plans, a variety of layouts are available to match the best physical accommodations to the nature and size of a work group. Typical rows of cubicles can be employed here, as long as the partition sizes fit the needs of the participants.

Typically, partitions of six feet or more provide a screen even when people are standing, requiring movement into adjoining areas if interactions are to take place. Screens of four feet or lower permit eye contact and conversations even while the occupants are seated, a potential bonus when interaction is desirable. Two or more cubicles can also be placed in pods or grouped arrangements with a shared central access point, also aimed at facilitating interaction among occupants.

Workstations provide another means of establishing team

areas. Grouped together along or around tables and separated from surrounding areas by tall partitions, this kind of arrangement is sometimes referred to as a bullpen because it enhances eye contact and verbal communication.

In some newer office layouts, companies have established hybrid applications of workspace, providing more than one kind of environment for different people to use as the need arises. This includes small group spaces that facilitate interaction, and isolated, acoustically-shielded retreats where individuals can go when they need to concentrate. This kind of application provides a balanced environment in which the individual moves to accommodate specific activities.

A private, enclosed office can also be used as a hybrid workspace. With the appropriate match, two employees may share this kind of space, provided it is the right size, thereby enhancing their interaction while still providing some separation from the bustle and distraction of more open space.

It is easy to picture the disadvantages of departments or groups of workers in large organizations who have frequent need to interact, but are separated by floors, wings, or even separate buildings. However, the majority of office space in the U.S. is not concentrated in large structures or complexes, but buildings of only 5,000 square feet or less, with an average size of a little more than 16,000 square feet. At this scale, the issue of proximity is more manageable, but often still a problem.

Accessibility is a vital component for effective work. This includes the proximity of individuals to others important to their work processes as well as the relative availability of equipment and resources.

In a survey from ASID, 68 percent of professionals (consultants, designers, etc.) working on office design projects reported improvements in productivity directly related to making people and resources more accessible. Some improvements may be as simple as placing group team members closer together or producing specialized workspaces that allow team members to collaborate. Accessibility projects may also involve producing schematics or floor plans that illustrate the links between employees and the people and equipment that they use regularly.

> *"Because physical space is a profound influencer of human behavior, small changes in the workplace can affect big changes in behavior and attitude: patterns of interaction, channels of communication, and development of relationships. These intangible forces may be stronger indicators of long-term business success than this quarter's financial results, and evaluation techniques for both tangible and intangible forces need to be employed."*
> — "Assessing Workplace Intangibles," Steelcase, 2000

EXECUTIVE SUMMARY
Office Size and Layout

There may be no such thing as an ideal office layout. In many modern business processes, changing work practices are the norm, requiring different uses of space over time. But there are basic needs that remain the same, including specialized spaces that match the needs of the activity taking place in them.

Existing office structures rarely provide the right mix or adaptability for any one tenant, making their use of space a continual compromise, reducing productivity.

New space represents an ideal opportunity for any organization to create the right atmosphere for effective work. The right number and size of meeting rooms, private offices, and open plan space can be developed, with each matching the known needs and anticipated growth.

Flexibility

"Space flexibility is increasingly more important than space efficiency. Investment in an office infrastructure that supports change and adaptability will pay long-term dividends."
— Eileen Circo (*Banker & Tradesman*, 6/1996)

Flexibility has become a trendy term in corporate conversations, but it is not a new concept. At its simplest, growth alone involves flexibility, and organizations have been growing as long as there have been organizations.

These days, however, the concept usually involves more than just traditional aspects of change. Flexibility is an ROI-related factor; strategies and tactics that deal with flexibility are critical to maintain market share and profitability, not just a means of staying in business.

Flexibility includes:

- business expansion
- business contraction
- project-based activity
- reorganization (management, divisions, workgroups)
- mergers and acquisitions
- relocation

Buildings have an impact on flexibility because they can impede or support the movement of personnel within a structure. Moving one or more people from one part of a room to another or from one floor to another used to require little more than a few boxes and a handcart.

These days, however, it is more likely to be a complex operation that includes rewiring phone and computer connections, reconfiguring network nodes, and often, training to deal with changes in protocols and formats for everything from computer formats to group communications. Furniture and equipment adjustments are also part of this mix, to deal with individual differences in height or handedness.

Even with buildings constructed within the last few decades, internal moves can pose physical problems. The biggest barriers are access to power and phone lines, with more than half of all moves creating problems in these areas.

Employees who are shuffled around a building frequently apparently do not suffer from a drop in productivity, according to a national research study by BOSTI. However, there is a direct relationship between the frequency of moves and job satisfaction. The fewer the moves, the greater the job satisfaction. Satisfaction with work groups also is related to relocation, with fewer moves linked to higher satisfaction with a group.

In the past few decades, many organizations have shifted to cubicle-based layouts in order to facilitate changes within an office. Flexibility can be enhanced with cubicles because, in many cases, the basic configuration and equipment remain in place; personnel move rather than fixtures. Minor adjustments may be all that is necessary to accommodate a new cubicle occupant.

"We believe technology, as a productivity facilitator, includes both automated machines and the work environment. The challenge to all of us is to coordinate and integrate the people, the space, and the technology of the office."

— William M. Hogan, *(Management Review, 3-1983)*

143

With the latest office furniture designs, flexibility is also a key issue. Although adjustable features may cost more initially, they allow for effective customization as different personnel move around. This had a direct impact on safety and health, because ergonomic effectiveness requires adjustments to take body size and working preferences into account. An added benefit is the element of control, a factor that a large majority of employees cite as important to their satifisfaction with their office environment and their effectiveness in it.

But simple shifts of existing personnel are only part of the picture. When a configuration of cubicles is arranged in an open office layout, it may be difficult to add more if personnel are to be added to a space. At the same time, reducing the number of occupants in a room may leave space wasted and unused because the same cubicle setup cannot be adjusted for the change.

And more complex changes within organizations may make existing cubicle usage even more unwieldy. Reorganizing a floor to create group clusters, for example, may leave little option but to shuffle workstations or cubicles into new pat-

Relocation Facts

1-2 relocations annually	28 percent
3-6 relocations annually	9 percent
total relocations annually	37 percent
relocations without moving the workspace	33 percent
average time lost per move, managers	14 hours
average time lost per move, clerical workers	2 hours
annual relocation rate for all workspaces other than private offices	15–25 percent
annual average relocation rate for managers and supervisors	20 percent
annual average relocation rate for non-supervisory workers	31 percent
annual average relocation rate for private sector workers	22 percent
annual average relocation rate for public sector workers	38 percent
annual average relocation rate for private offices	16 percent
annual average relocation rate for open offices/bullpens	31–34 percent

[BOSTI]

terns, limiting or eliminating more efficient layouts where interactive work — typically generating more conversations and noise — can be isolated from areas where individuals need acoustic privacy. To allow the most flexible options, a

Elements of Flexibility

- amount of floor space
- number and movability of room dividers and walls
- ceiling height
- HVAC expandability
- telecommunications expandability
- access and adapability for new telecommunications
- power availability and access
- room and task lighting
- individual workspace design
- adjustable furniture and fixtures for left- and right-handedness, height, and weight
- file storage accessibility and movability
- access to shared equipment/features
- accomodations for persons with disabilities

building design requires more than just large open spaces because modern office furniture is often more flexible than the buildings it is used in.

Many existing office structures have fixed layouts that limit the ability to group people or create smaller team environments. When a building consists only of enclosed offices, the only flexibility option is to shuffle people among fixed locations. When a building consists only of open spaces, the only option is to shuffle the arrangement of room dividers or cubicles.

For most organizations, there may be no single ideal mix of space between enclosed offices, meeting rooms, and open office areas. Too much or too little of one may impede flexibility in the future, but with thoughtful analysis at the beginning, an appropriate mix will allow the most number of alternatives in the future.

> *"Each time management restructures, new technologies are introduced, people switch projects, or priorities shift, it impacts how people get their jobs done."*
>
> — Pam Brenn
> Manager of Workplace Issues, Steelcase

Flexibility

If change is a fundamental reality of today's business structure, then office space should provide the adaptability to match the change. Space that is hampered by fixed structural elements, lack of connectivity, poor HVAC service, or other limits represents a barrier to growth.

Ideal office space should provide quick and affordable changes, permitting the shift of personnel and the reassignment of teams as strategy dictates. Especially with communications technology — wireless networks, local computer networks, and the Internet — work space must take into account both the current standards and those that are on the horizon.

Safety and Security

*"Virtually every type of building design —
from multifamily to mixed use to retail and
office — is being reassessed as architects and
clients focus on ways to heighten security.
The challenge is to strike a balance between
appealing architectural design and safety
measures that avoids turning buildings into
fortresses."* — *Christina Gair*
(National Real Estate Institute Online, 2/2002)

The outside world represents a growing threat to both public and private sector organizations. Although terrorism may top the paranoia list for most consumers, there are plenty of other daily problems that present a security threat to employees, from email viruses to random thefts.

In most office environments, employees do not have a major ongoing fear of violent attacks. This attitude is partly based on reality; the majority of businesses have never experienced an act of violence on site. Yet some fear does exist, particularly in locations within urban neighborhoods where the reality of daily life includes the presence of criminals, hostility, and the potential of random violence.

Less inside than outside, office workers expect the business environment to provide basic protection against at least the most common kinds of unwanted problems, including vandalism, theft, and molestation. This kind of security may be as simple as adequate lighting for parking and access areas, but it can also extend to appropriate designs for the use of sites. Although existing buildings may not provide this kind of solution, new buildings increasingly include security as a designed-in element of exterior use of space.

Parking areas, for example, can be sited to provide the shortest, most visible avenues of approach, with ample lighting, fencing, and lines of sight. Doorways and entrance areas can also be designed to minimize shadows and hidden nooks where criminals can lurk. Large organizations may have the budget support for full-time security personnel to complement defensive design strategies, but even smaller businesses can benefit from a security-minded design when building new facilities, especially the use of built-in sensors and alarm systems that can accommodate a variety of work schedules.

"On-the-job tension stemming from rising layoffs and crashing retirement accounts is fueling an increase in workplace violence."

— *Business Insurance* (5/12/2003)

New government buildings now require a higher level of structural protection, a consequence of the bombing of the federal building in Oklahoma City. Even smaller district buildings have guidelines dealing with controlled access, underground parking, setbacks from property lines, blast-proof windows, and other elements. The average corporate building may not be interested in nor need such features, but if needed, these are much easier to deal with in new construction than a retrofit, if possible at all.

Other aspects of safety that can help ease employee fears include clear management policies, training sessions, working procedures to deal with access after hours, and ongoing maintenance to handle lighting and lock problems. Office designs can also incorporate interior features that offer protection, including safe rooms, lockable offices, secured storage areas, and panic switches.

Security Factors

Security threats in the office environment:

- computer attacks (email viruses, hacking, and internal misuse)
- internal theft
- external theft
- burglaries and robberies
- arson
- violent crime
- vandalization

Security features in the office environment:

- alarm systems
- external door locks
- internal door locks
- window security
- employee identification
- visitor identification
- access control at main entrance
- access control at secondary entrances
- perimeter security for site
- parking lot security
- shipping and receiving security
- records and files security

For all sizes of businesses, day-to-day operations are increasingly dependent on computers and high-speed data connections to the outside world. Given this reality, security plans and infrastructure should include the ability to maintain operations even when the power is out, the function of uninterruptible back-up power systems. Particularly during "mission critical" activities, the ability to stay online and powered up is crucial and some kinds of businesses may avoid leasing space in areas where power outages are a frequent occurrence.

Security includes designs and planning for non-criminal threats, such as dealing with severe weather, power outages,

Architecural Safety and Security Features

Elements of architectural designs that are related to safety and security:

- width of exit stairs
- mechanical smoke inhalation devices
- firefighter communications systems
- blast resistance
- public access to lobbies
- secondary access
- emergency signage
- emergency lighting
- backup power
- floor surfaces

road closures, and fire. The best defense against such a wide range of potential dangers is to start with a building design that allows occupants as much protection as possible as well as the simplest, safest means of escape.

In new buildings, integrated systems can combine communications, sensors, and alarms, improving the ability to detect and deal with problems as they arise. The latest applications with this kind of integration also add connections to the Internet and closed circuit TV capabilities. The former can be used for access to monitors, sensors, and switching from remote locations; the latter allows quick and flexible video nodes as they are needed to deal with situations or changes in building use.

Although secondary to the value of personnel, the protection of assets should also be included in security policies and designs. For most organizations today, much of what they do is dependent on computers and digital information. Protecting digital files thus becomes a major component of security.

Software is the main tool for online protection, and this is independent of the structure of a building. But hard drives, tape and disk storage, and other forms of digital archives represent formats that are often housed within a building and subject to attacks, theft, and damage. Buildings can incorporate safe rooms, vaults, or other structural elements designed to safeguard these assets without impeding access for daily use.

Workplace violence, a major factor contributing to the perception of safety and security in the workplace, is a difficult activity to measure. There are no authoritative conclusions as to whether or not it is increasing, but there is certainly enough to warrant attention. Between 1993 and 1999, for example, the Bureau of Justice Statistics reported more than one million episodes of violence in U.S. workplaces, and the National Institute for the Prevention of Workplace Violence estimates that the cost of this kind of violence is about $36 billion annually.

Workplace violence is primarily an issue associated with Human Resource management. But merely because it exists, it has an impact on employees' feeling of security, a factor that may require some applications to the design and functions of buildings.

Safety issues related to the potential harm of office equipment and layouts may seem like a trivial issue, because physical injuries are most often thought of as something related to factories, assembly lines, and manual labor. But injuries are also commonplace in office envrionments, some of them related to characteristics of building design, such as floors and walls, implicated in slips, falls, and impacts.

A bigger issue, however, is repetitive stress injuries, also known as cumulative trauma disorders, which include the well-publicized carpal tunnel syndrome. More than half of all workers' compensation claims involve these kind of problems, although many are still associated with repetitive work done in factories or shops. Because of the growing dependency on computer keyboards, as many as half of all office workers may be suceptible to these ailments.

Most repetitive injury problems in offices can be addressed by appropriate use of ergonomic equipment and furniture, not something directly related to office layout and design. But there is a link, because lighting can be a factor, such as forcing improper postures to block screen glare on computers; another factor can be use of existing space that has built-in limitations preventing the use of modern, appropriately-designed furniture or fixtures.

This is an area worthy of attention by companies because of proof that it provides results. The U.S. Army Corps of Engineers, for example, reported a 21 percent improvement in employee productivity following a shift to ergonomic furniture. A university study (Miami University, Ohio) also reported such improvements, between 15 and 27 percent, after ergonomic changes had been made.

> *"Increased productivity occurs when people perform tasks more accurately, faster, without loss of accuracy, for longer time periods, without getting tired. The same is true when people can learn more effectively, are more creative, can sustain stress more effectively, work together more harmoniously, and are more able to cope with unforeseen circumstances."*
>
> — Ossama A. Abdou
> *(Journal of Architectural Engineering)*

EXECUTIVE SUMMARY
Safety and Security

In recent years, violence and crime in the work place have shifted from being abstractions to a cause of daily concern. From international terrorism to armed robbery, offices are no longer considered safe harbors by those that work in them.

Organizations must deal with employee paranoia as well as more concrete economic pressures, such as the increasing cost of insurance, that are linked to security and safety in their buildings. Although there may be no direct threat from terrorists in the average office, there is an ongoing battle to limit liability from more localized problems, including vandalism, theft, computer hacking, and sexual assault. Slips and falls, injuries with office equipment, fire, and other safety issues add importance to this subject.

Buildings themselves can provide an important defense against both crime and accidents, with lighting, floor surfaces, access points, sensors, and alarms part of a wide set of practical tools that can be employed. As always, there is added cost — and disruptions — involved with adding these elements to existing buildings.

Sustainability and Green Buildings

"Companies and institutions with vision, a socially conscious operating philosophy and substantial resources are making investments for the long haul in the form of entirely green buildings or campuses. While choosing to build green may drive up initial construction costs by as much as an additional $50 per square foot, these companies and institutions have faith that paying the hefty green premium in the short term will provide immediate benefits as well as long-term savings."

— Jim Lorick (*Metropolis Magazine*, 2003)

How can the environmental impact of an office building have an impact on employee effectiveness? By addressing a complex of situations that affect job satisfaction, indoor air quality, community impact, energy use, and other factors that help develop and maintain the health of a business.

Sustainability is the key term used to represent how environmentally sensitive a building is, from construction through longevity. Properly implemented, the concept begins with a design appropriate for a site and use, able to accommodate future changes and needs, and making the most efficient use of materials and energy. The location and siting of a building, for example, can be adjusted to take greatest advantage of natural features, provide the most effective orientation to the sun for use of solar energy, and provide the best fit with existing neighborhood resources.

157

According to the Office of the Federal Environmental Executive, green building is defined as "the practice of increasing the efficiency with which buildings and their sites use energy, water, and materials, and reducing building impacts on human health and the environment, through better siting, design, construction, operation, maintenance and removal through the complete building life cycle."

During construction, green design principles include selecting materials from locations that have the shortest distance for shipping — decreasing the use of fuel during transportation while helping support local suppliers — and making the most efficient use of them during construction, reducing waste. And for excess material and waste that is generated, a sustainability plan includes reducing the amount that ends up in landfills. Like many sustainability factors, this has environmental as well as economic benefits. Less waste equals less cost.

Buildings designed with sustainable characteristics focus on reducing energy use. With the most effective orientation, heating costs can be reduced; design features can also reduce the amount of unwanted solar heat gain. This reduces ongoing energy use and cost as well as allowing smaller, less expensive HVAC systems to be specified.

Windows and daylighting are a key element of sustainability, emphasizing a traditional building feature that lost favor during decades of energy-saving activities. With the latest thermal glass products, sunlight can provide the highest quality interior lighting without compromising comfort.

Building materials are also a major component of sustainable design. Renewable materials — brick, wood, etc. — as well as laminates, recycled products, steel, and concrete pro-

The LEED™ system

The U.S. Green Building Council was founded in 1993, the concept of David Gottfried, a developer, and Michael Italiano, an environmental lawyer. Functioning as a nonprofit organization, the USGBC develops and runs the primary rating system for green buildings, the Leadership in Energy and Environmental Design Green Building Rating Program, better known as the LEED™ program.

A point system is used to qualify buildings in one of four levels, Certified, Silver, Gold, or Platinum. The greater the number of points — and the higher the rank — the greater the energy savings and environmental benefits. As of 2003, more than 3,300 companies, agencies, and organizations belonged to the USGBC, with the majority (more than 2,200) being companies working in construction, design, or other building-related professions.

About 1,000 buildings have been registered as LEED™ structures to date, with federal, state, and local governments representing almost half of the listings.

vide a wide variety of options for architects and engineers, with the goal of reducing or removing objectionable consequences such as VOCs.

Lighting and HVAC provide the heart of the sustainable building concept. The goal of high quality lighting systems is to provide the right kind of light for the right tasks, eliminating energy waste, with both individual controls and centralized automation. Lighting, as previously discussed, has a direct impact on human performance in the office environment and is an ongoing target for reducing maintenance and usage costs.

In combination with daylighting, the overall use of electricity for this function can be cut while the quality of the output is improved.

Sustainable buildings should not sacrifice personal comfort for energy savings, and they don't. Design, appropriate materials, adequate insulation and sealing, and efficient HVAC systems make modern sustainable buildings as comfortable or more so than comparable, non-sustainable structures. Just as with proper lighting, there are multiple winners; employee satisfaction and effectiveness is increased and the cost of heating and cooling is reduced.

Budget logic supports sustainable office designs, even though the initial cost of the design and some components may be more than for a traditional structure. This is because the added expense of certain materials, technologies, and design elements yield long-term savings in operations and improved productivity by employees. Even if a build-to-suit

Case Study

Site. EPA District 7 Science & Technology center (Kansas City, KS).

Project. A new 72,000 square foot office building with a Gold level LEED™ rating. Goals: advanced energy efficiency, water conservation, resource conservation, and high IAQ.

Results. Maximum energy savings of 54 percent, 72 percent diversion of construction debris, estimated 763,000 gallons of water/year supplied by rooftop rainwater collection system.

project does not set out to be registered as sustainable, the selection of energy-efficient components will create the same result in part because of the reduced use of energy.

Sustainability also provides an added level of benefit that most employees and organizations recognize as noteworthy. A building can be merely a place to house workers while performing functions that generate a profit, but without an added level of identity, it has lost a critical opportunity. Buildings can create or magnify identities, providing a specific look and concrete impression to both the outside world and the work culture within. In general, studies show that buildings provide a more important statement when an organization has significant public contact. In most other cases, the building represents more substance — conservative use of shareholder funds and the ability to attract and retain employees — than image.

A sustainable building provides a unique signature in both look and substance, generating additional pride of place. One proof of this is in the publicity that existing sustainable buildings have received. Not only are their physical characteristics exploited, the building images are profiled, helping company be branded with their unique look.

What is the major barrier to building green buildings? Cost. Although there are some energy-saving components of building design that add little or no additional costs, most of the features associated with environmentally-sensitive structures add to the expenditures, both in the design and construction stages. Based on the LEED™ system, at least one study has linked added expenditures to the various rating levels associated with this program, but this extra spending is often site specific. LEED™ rating in itself also costs money, a fixed fee, and usually requires the participation of one or more accredit-

Green Thinking

In a recent survey by the International Facility Management Association, 95 percent of facility professionals reported that they believed sustainability is becoming a more important issue.

"Green" factors already part of facilities:

- use of natural daylight   78 percent
- lighting fixture retrofits   67 percent
- use of recycled office products   67 percent
- light sensors   58 percent
- water conservation   48 percent
- high performance windows   44 percent
- Energy Star program   33 percent

ed professionals during design and construction phases, also a potential for added cost.

In general, a formal environmental rating goal such as LEED™ could add 1 to 5 percent overall to the initial construction costs of a new structure. These costs are also dropping over time, reflecting the rapid increase in professional support and expertise available, competition, acquired knowledge that can be applied to traditional construction techniques, and lower costs for appropriate materials and equipment.

But this program and others, such as the EPA's Energy Star ratings, also reflect another realistic goal, return on investment. Added expenditures associated with equipment, materials, or planning aimed at reducing energy costs pay for themselves in the long run, sometimes in only a matter of months or a few years.

And buildings that have been designed to be energy efficient typically provide an indoor environment that is more comfortable to a larger number of occupants, reducing complaints, heath problems, and absenteeism. Plus, since green buildings typically involve more daylighting than other convential building designs, there are added psychological and productivity factors because of the benefits this feature provides.

> *"Energy-efficient building and office design offers the possibility of significantly increased worker productivity. By improving lighting, heating, and cooling, workers can be made more comfortable and productive. An increase of 1 percent in productivity can provide savings to a company that exceed its entire energy bill. Efficient design practices are cost-effective just from their energy savings; the resulting productivity gains make them indispensable."*
>
> — Rocky Mountain Institute
> (*"Greening the Building and the Bottom Line"*)

Sustainability and Green Buildings

It is easy for building owners and managers to be cynical about the green building movement. Not because of a lack of concern for environmental issues, but because sustainability in the building industry has a reputation for costliness.

Green buildings, especially those designed with industry standards (such as the LEED™ rating system), do typically cost more than comparable structures with the same amount of space, but they also offer substantial rewards.

Environmentally compatible offices are universally admired as providing high quality working environments and they also offer a more tangible ROI, quick paybacks for the energy-saving features they employ.

Decision Factors: Building a User Effective™ Office

"In terms of dollar outlay over the 40-year life cycle of an office building, 2–3 percent is generally spent on the initial costs of the building and equipment; 6–8 percent on maintenance and replacement; and 90–92 percent is generally spent on personnel salaries and benefits. These data suggest that if an investment in physical planning and design could be made that would favorably influence organizational effectiveness and therefore reduce personnel costs, total life-cycle costs could be substantially reduced."

— Jean Wineman (*Behavioral Issues in Office Design*)

As a general rule of thumb, the nature of the office space will not guarantee that a business will succeed. In fact, many businesses succeed despite limitations in their workspace. Many very successful businesses start out in very undesirable space — Microsoft, as one example, began in a garage — but over time, the enthusiasm and energy associated with a start-up phase, necessary to overcome barriers, is replaced by more sober day-to-day realities. In the long run, issues such as the temperature of an office, the quality of the indoor air, and who sits where have a direct impact on success and failure.

To the building owner or tenant, the workspace itself is a potent tool, hampering or boosting the activities that generate

The Role of an Office Building

The effectiveness of an office building is related to its functions. Despite the wide range of activities and sizes, offices share several primary goals.

- to facilitate the interaction between employees and the information they need to do their job

- to facilitate interaction between employees in order that they accomplish their work

- to facilitate interaction between employees and the equipment and technology they need to accomplish their jobs

profits. According to more than a decade of recent research by BOSTI Associates, the effect of the workplace varies in several important categories that define employment. It has the greatest effect on job satisfaction — with 24 percent of the influence compared to 76 percent from pay — advancement opportunities, managerial direction, and other inputs.

Next in importance is team performance, where 11 percent of the influence comes from the workplace and 89 percent from the other factors. With individual performance, 5 percent of the influence is due to the workplace and 95 percent from other factors.

If workplace influence is not the dominant factor, why should it be addressed? Because it costs relatively little compared to overall personnel costs, produces an immediate payback, and has a long-lasting effect.

Of those components of the workplace that have the greatest impact on all three categories — jobs satisfaction, team performance, and personal performance — the most important are:

- workplaces that permit concentration and limit or eliminate distractions
- environments supportive of informal interactions with other workers, a situation that encourages learning and keeping current

What must an organization do to determine the effectiveness of its office space? Some answers may already be well known, through verbal or written evidence that occupants recognize specific elements as problem areas. This includes complaints about the temperature, health problems blamed on IAQ, noise distractions, glare from overhead lighting, and wasted time spent getting to copy machines or meeting rooms. These factors can also be identified and measured with employee surveys or the use of consultants specializing in the office environment.

> *"It's not just about opportunities anymore. Facilities show how the company feels about you. Are you valued or are you seen as someone who can easily be replaced? Facilities are becoming a key point for attracting and retaining workers."*
> — Gary Wheeler (Perkins & Will)

The use of space is a trickier factor to quantify, but it, too, can be identified with some simple tools, including surveys and observation. In general, even though employees may be quick to gripe about apparently insignificant things, they are also the best resource when it comes to determining how they do their jobs.

For most organizations, how much space is needed is as important, or more so, than how the space is used. Here, too,

167

Building Impacts

Executives identify and rank key decision factors when deciding to build a new office structure, as reported in a recent national survey [Center for the Built Environment]

1. **Site and Building.** Where and what to build, including the appropriate functions for a new building, its size, and how it is to be configured.

2. **Infrastructure.** Types and components for HVAC, telecommunications, electrical, lighting, acoustics, and energy efficiency.

3. **Image and Add-ons.** Specific design related to the corporate image, and additional features desired, including parking, security, meeting facilities, and access to transportation.

Less important, generally considered as advantageous but not necessarily practical or affordable

4. **Flexibility and Alternatives.** Design features incorporating flexwork, hoteling, telecommuting, teamwork, and future strategies.

5. **Sustainability.** Occupant comfort, recycling, environmentally-friendly functions, energy savings, LEED™ certification, and corporate image.

---

simple formulas or guidelines can be helpful in establishing appropriate measurements, such as the space needed for data entry or management functions.

With basic information about space use established, the most difficult task follows, determining what kind of new space represents the best use of financial resources. At the simplest level, this means a decision to lease space in an existing building, either as is or with remodeling. The alternative of a build-to-suit structure, however, can provide a strategic advantage, with an appropriate economic edge over the long term.

In the past, the decision to build a new office building has usually been associated with larger companies, not small ones. It is not just economics at play here, however. Although larger companies may have more fiscal clout and more familiarity with making decisions involving larger amounts of money, they also are more likely to need large amounts of space. Not just custom-designed workspaces, but enough existing space to fit their needs, something harder to find in the typical commercial real estate market.

Small companies, on the other, hand, not only are more likely to find usable space available, but are less likely to have a corporate culture that links its identity to a building. For this end of the market — mostly privately-held corporations — price is more important than other benefits. But no matter what the size, all businesses have something to gain by examining their use of workspace and the potential gains achievable when the space fits the needs and performs its functions efficiently.

Business Costs

Total cost of a business office over 10 years (total is more than 100 percent due to rounding):

facilities	5 percent	
operations	4 percent	
technology	10 percent	
personnel	82 percent	[BOSTI]

Automated Advantages

According to a study by the National Instutute of Standards and Technology, there are numerous benefits to be gained from automated building systems, including:

- fewer false alarms for fire/safety systems
- improved safety and efficiency for fire and rescue responses
- lower risk of injuries/fatalities during emergencies
- reduced property losses during fire events
- lower risk of building-related illnesses
- lower energy costs
- improved control of temperature, humidity, and lighting
- improved indoor air quality
- fewer lost workdays
- increased occupant comfort
- decreased down time
- less occupant turnover
- improved diagnosis/trouble-shooting capabilities
- improved management of unoccupied space
- longer equipment life
- lower repair/replacement costs for equipment
- lower operations/maintenance costs
- reduction in insurance costs
- reduced waste/pollution
- faster commissioning/start-up operations

Among all sizes of businesses, the building that hosts the business plays a noticeable role in the image of the organization. In its national survey of office tenants, BOMA and the Urban Land Institute reported that "tenants want their buildings to look good inside and out and to convey the right image."

Of those companies surveyed, 77 percent stated that building image and prestige are of "the highest importance," and more than 80 percent of respondents ranked the exterior, entry lobby, common areas, and grounds as "very important."

Mid-sized and large corporations are more likely to identify buildings as essential parts of their corporation identity. In this end of the market, the cost of a building is tied to payback and the ratio of benefits to cost. Yet the "look and feel" of a business structure plays an important role in its success, no matter the size.

> *"Productivity is and always will be the most important issue in business. Organizations that produce an attractive rate of return on investment prosper, those that don't fail. From this purely functional perspective, people are processing units creating outputs from inputs. Whether it be manufacturing or knowledge work, the issue is the same. Productivity is organizational effectiveness."*
> — Wayne Morrow
> (Intellibuild 95

Clients and competitors consciously and unconsciously rate a building; the building itself can add or detract from the stature of its occupants. And if it has no effect whatsoever — neither client nor competitor even notices the building — what might that suggest about lost opportunities?

Intelligent Buildings

Offices that are considered "intelligent buildings" generally share the following characteristics, according to surveys by BOMA and the Urban Land Institute.

- fiber optics
- built-in Internet connections
- high-speed network wiring
- LAN and WAN connectivity
- satellite accessibility
- ISDN access
- redundant power source
- built-in conduits for power, data, and phone cables
- energy-efficient HVAC system
- automated lighting system
- smart elevators
- automated lavatory fixtures
- computerized building directory

In the job market, a building can also perform a valuable function. At least when a prospective employee has more than one option for employment, studies indicate that the company with a more attractive building may gain an edge, even if this is not the deciding factor.

Looks aside, one of the most significant decision support factors with all sizes of business is value. Cost by itself is important, but more so in the perspective of what an expenditure produces. This can be considered a "return on investment" or payback and, ultimately, it represents value.

With a building, value varies in definition from one element to another — indoor air quality may be more important than appearance or flexible suite layouts more important than covered parking — as well from one owner or tenant to another. Differences in how buildings are used provides one rationale for this variation, because a high tech development office will have different needs from a call center or an insurance agency.

Surveys of useful building components point to a separation between elements that are necessary and those that are desirable. In the former category are HVAC systems that provide comfortable working conditions, healthy indoor air quality, high quality building maintenance, and power capacity, among others.

The latter category represents more of a "wish list," and includes fiber optics, built-in wiring for the Internet, satellite accessibility, automated lighting and HVAC controls, raised flooring for flexibility, and other elements often related to the "intelligent building" trend. But though companies may

---

Building Needs

When analyzing the need for a move, including the decision to lease or build to suit, the most important evaluation criteria are:

- functionality
- cost and ROI
- corporate philosophy and culture
- competition in the market
- market cycle of the corporation
- location

---

express interest in the intelligent building elements, unless they are convinced of the value (payback, ROI), they are usually unwilling to pay extra for them.

In recent years, industry surveys have indicated a general lack of interest in intelligent office buildings because potential tenants do not know about or grasp the value of such systems. That is, the higher initial costs are not explored or justified for the savings they can produce long term. Intelligent building components such as automated lighting systems and high-tech HVAC controls are also shunned because of the expected "learning curve" for their installation and maintenance.

One trend expected in the near future is the expansion of intelligent building characteristics to automate more functions

Return on People (ROP)

Executives and managers increasingly rely on the concept of ROI — Return on Investment — to support decisions for equipment purchases, software upgrades, mergers and acquisitions, and many other critical elements related to being in business and generating a profit. ROI provides a key analytical tool for comparing leasing options, tax liabilities, depreciation, and productivity, among others.

But in most modern businesses, the majority of assets are not linked to physical objects, but people, ideas, and information. Plus, most of the cost of running a business is not associated with material things, but salaries.

Therefore, it makes sense to invest in the appropriate support to make this people-based asset perform most effectively. This includes training, salaries, support services, and high quality management, as well as the physical environment in which people work.

and provide less expensive, modular components that conform to industry standards. Just as computerized components became more common — and much less expensive — in automobiles in the 1980s and 1990s, computers will carve an affordable role for themselves in a wider range of applications in commercial buildings. This trend will also include more capabilities for quick diagnosis of building problems, as Internet links are already being designed to allow remote access for analysis.

Many of the wiring challenges that now impede upgrades and improvements to existing buildings are also expected to diminish even as the number and variety of devices, sensors, and switches needing to be connected multiplies. The alternative to more wires is wireless connectivity. Already the hottest growth area for home networking and portable electronic devices — based on the WiFi and Bluetooth standards — this kind of broadcast link allows quick "plug and use" capabilities.

> *"Good facility design requires a systems or ecological view from the beginning. This means considering the nature of technology, management style and organization practices, use policies, facility design and work practices as interdependent components. The system is not likely to prosper, or even survive, unless all these factors are working in harmony."*
>
> — Becker, Sims, Davis
> *(Managing Space Efficiently)*

In commercial applications, unlike the home, however, business needs will require more attention to encrypted signals to avoid giving away useful information to competitors or hackers, always lurking on the fringes of the latest advances.

Measures of Effectiveness

- total cost of space per employee
- total occupancy cost per square foot
- utilization rate (floor space per person)
- ratio of real property cost to total budget
- rental cost per square foot
- operating cost per square foot
- occupant/tenant satisfaction rate
- percent vacant space
- absenteeism rate
- churn rate
- revenues per square foot
- revenues per employee
- net income per square foot
- net income per employee
- gross profit per square foot
- gross profit per employee
- occupancy cost as percentage of revenue (or expenses or income)

Larger buildings also may have some built-in disadvantages that may not pose a problem in residential buildings, structural elements that block wireless signals. But as this technology quickly advances, solutions are also being created to deal with such difficulties.

Another potent argument for utilizing effective workspaces also hinges on improved productivity. A reduced staff and improved retention — both achievable outcomes with the proper office design — yields more financial flexibility in the choice of space and location. In recent years, some corporations that have downsized have taken the opportunity to leverage their increased productivity in upgraded facilities.

In some cases, this has resulted in upgrades of leased space, jumping from Class-B buildings to Class-A without a greater expenditure because less space is needed overall. The same logic can apply to organizations as part of a build-to-suit plan, selecting locations, building styles, and office amenities that would not be affordable on a larger scale.

Since the 1970s, the North America office market has rapidly adapted to open rooms using cubicles for individual employees. In a way, this has become a corporate trend and organizations sometimes choose to shift their workforces into this kind of workspace — or more often, a mix of cubicles and private offices — more to "keep up with the Joneses" than as a result of careful study.

Like it or not, cubicles are now a significant part of the office scene because they do provide benefits, at least for some kinds of employees and some kinds of work activities. But there is some evidence that when companies move employees from private offices to open space, their productivity drops, and some leave — sooner or later — to take other jobs, ones that restore them to the private space they are used to.

Effectiveness Defined

In some offices, some work may involve the processing of forms, other paperwork, or client information, activities that can be measured in terms of output per unit of time. Much of the time, however, the work of modern offices is less easy to measure, making productivity a complicated factor. In general, the effectiveness of an office may require the analysis of several key areas in order to determine the effects of changes.

profitability	the difference between revenue and cost
quality	how closely output comes to specifications or expectations
efficiency	the relationship between performance and resources used during performance
productivity	the relationship between output and the resources used to produce it (time, materials, etc.)

Radical shifts that include moving people into open space can succeed, however, with the right amount of communication and allowing workers to participate in some of the decisions that are part of the move, such as personalizing spaces, selecting furniture, etc. Another component that has been successful during these kinds of move is coordinating them with education and training programs that reorganize business processes and activities. In this effort, everyone is included to reduce potential feelings of unfairness.

There is also growing dissatisfaction with open-plan offices among some of the early adopters of the format. It is not just that the atmosphere is alien to some workers, but that it is more conducive to interaction than concentration, and many kinds of work activity require the latter, not the former.

Hierarchies are also part of the criticism of open plan office space. The traditional responsibilities and authority that managers and executives have are ill-suited to the egalitarianism of open space rooms. Status is a recognizable element in office

What Influences Productivity

Various studies estimate that employee productivity can be increased between 10 and 20 percent due to the features of high quality buildings. The features of buildings have an important effect on how their occupants perform, but the effect varies from feature to feature and even from person to person.

Among the factors affecting individual productivity:

- technical competence
- motivation and personality
- job satisfaction
- attitude
- leadership
- organizational structure
- workflow
- equipment, technology, and technical support
- personal relationships
- type of occupation
- indoor environment

culture and may need to be supported with the appropriate office space assignments, yet work activities by higher level employees also often require more privacy, supporting their need for this kind of perk.

In reality, many businesses must now divide the use of space as much because of economic considerations as tradition or status. In most cases, floor space is too expensive to give every employee a private office; there must be some variety to accommodate supply with demand.

But as the average cubicle size shrinks, realities also suggest

Overcoming

"People factors" play a significant role in the quest for improvements in an office environment. Even the tiniest things can make a difference, at least where behavior and productivity are concerned.

Many of us teeter between the gritty need to just get through the day and our lofty intentions to really do the job right. Frequently, what sends us careening down the wrong path are the myriad environmental frictions that make the right thing just a little too inconvenient a little too often.

The typical office is rife with these frictions. The file credenza that's attractively placed — but across the room — means that records pile up on the desk, instead of getting filed. The sales assistant who's stationed down the hall means that sales reps get wrapped up in "administrivia" instead of sales calls. A scarcity of meeting space means that off-the-cuff collaborations happen less often, and less proactively. Bottom line: The reason that there is no such thing as a good generic office is because there is no such thing as generic work.

Urging employees to work with what they've got is useless. In the long run, most people will take the path of least resistance that more businesses will have to pay attention to some of the drawbacks of the open-space scenarios because packing more workers into the same space can backfire. Loss of privacy, noise distractions, lack of space, and other factors not only have a negative impact on productivity, they increase absenteeism and turnover.

If there is a single conclusion from a decade or more of research about the new realities of office space, it is that there is no single formula that works best. Each organization depends on a mix of business activities and range of employees that

---

Friction

most of the time. Fortunately, today's best workplace designers can help. Good design removes the little frictions that discourage productivity. But good design must be informed.

Designers need to understand the work for which they are designing. They need to know what equipment will be used, by which employees, and how often. They need to know who interacts with whom, and how. In short, they need to understand the work processes, both formal and informal.

That understanding of work processes can only come from a serious management effort to document processes. This will inevitably mean talking with employees who do the work, rather than managers who think they know the work. Of course, this exercise is a sterling opportunity to improve processes, as well.

Understanding one's own work processes, and communicating them, isn't a trivial undertaking. But it does make for a much more productive partnership with designers, which means a much more productive workplace.

—William Casey, Ph.D.
Executive Leadership Group www.elg.net

---

necessitates a specific use of space in order to maximize effectiveness. In general, economic pressures may be driving more companies to open plan layouts — allowing a higher density of employees per square foot — but how the open space is used, and the relationship with the amount of space dedicated to traditional private offices, should be determined on a case by case basis.

This conlusion is summed up in "Managing Space Efficiently," a report from the International Facility Management Program at Cornell University. "The best approaches to managing space efficiently balance, consciously and formally, the need to reduce costs with the need to enhance employee effectiveness." In most cases, it costs more money and the results are less certain when the space in question is in an existing structure. Aging components, outdated equipment, and the restrictions imposed by existing structural elements work against the ideal model of space usage.

To generate the most effective use of space, the ideal solution would be a new structure, one designed and built from scratch to meet an organization's specific needs. Any organization, no matter the size, should consider this option as a potent objective whenever office space is being considered.

"Make people more comfortable; they become happier, they work more efficiently, their bosses are happy, and their bosses' bosses are happier. And, if it looks good, then everyone is happy."

— Susan Boyle ("Value-Driven Design," *Buildings Magazine*, 10-2003)

EXECUTIVE SUMMARY

User Effective™ Buildings

In just about any component of an office building, something can be done to improve workflow, communications, employee satisfaction and other variables that impact profits. People are as much an asset as structure; removing barriers that impede their work provides a solid, measurable return on investment. In the case of old, obsolete, or inefficient buildings, the removal of these barriers may be impractical, disruptive, or just plain expensive. Moving to another existing building to escape problems may also generate unintended difficulties, and it is unlikely that any existing building provides the most efficient match to an organization's activity needs.

A practical alternative is to design and build a new building, balancing size and features with needs and budgets. In the context of the elements explored in this book, a build-to-suit office is an investment that provides important dividends for both employees and budgets.

Resources

American Institute of Architects (industry group/Washington, DC) 202-626-7300 www.aia.org

American Productivity and Quality Center (industry group/ Houston, TX) 713-681-4020 www.apqc.org

American Society of Heating, Refrigerating and Air-Conditioning Engineers (industry group/Atlanta, GA) 404-636-8400 www.ashrae.org

American Society of Interior Designers (industry group/ Washington, DC) 202-675-2371 www.asid.org

Architectural Record (periodical/New York, NY) 212-904-2594 www.archrecord.construction.com

BOSTI (Buffalo Organization for Social and Technological Innovation) Associates (consulting, research/Buffalo, NY) 716-837-7120 www.bosti.com

Building Environment Division/Building and Fire Research Laboratory/National Institute of Standards and Technology (research/Beltsville, MD) 301-975-5850 www.bfrl.nist.gov/863/bed.html

Building Design & Construction (periodical/Oak Brook, IL) 630-288-8153 www.bdcmag.com

Buildings Magazine (periodical/Cedar Rapids, IA) 319-364-6167 www.buildings.com

Building Green Inc. (information, support/Brattleboro, VT) 802-257-7300 www.buildinggreen.com

Building Owners and Managers Association (industry group/ Washington, DC) 202-408-2662 www.boma.org

Buildings Topics/Energy Efficiency and Renewable Energy/U.S. DOE (government resource/ www.eere.energy.gov/EE/buildings.html

Center for the Built Environment/University of California (research/Berkeley, CA) 510-642-49850 www.cbe.berkeley.edu

Construction Engineering Research Laboratory/U.S. Army Corps of Engineers (research/Champaign, IL) 800-872-2375

Construction Specifications Institute (industry group/ Alexandria, VA) 800-689-2900 www.csinet.org

Cool Roof Rating Council (industry group/Oakland, CA) 866-465-2523 www.coolroofs.org

Corporate Design Foundation (industry group/Boston, MA) 617-350-7097 www.cdf.org

Early Office Museum (research, information/New York, NY) www.officemuseum.com

Energy Star Program/U.S. EPA (government resource/ Washington, DC) 888-782-7937 www.energystar.gov

Executive Leadership Group (consulting/Lakewood, CO) 720-963-9212 www.elg.net

FMLink (online periodical) www.fmlink.com

Human Factors and Ergonomics Society (industry group/ Santa Monica, CA) 310-394-1811 www.hfes.org

Greenguard Environmental Institute (standards, certification/ Atlanta, GA) 800-427-9681 www.greenguard.org

Green Seal (industry group/Washington, DC) 202-872-6400 www.greenseal.org

Haworth Furniture, Inc. (office furniture/Holland, MI) 800-344-2600 www.haworth.com

Heating/Piping/AirConditioning Engineering (periodical/ Cleveland, OH) 216-696-3432 www.hpac.com

Herman Miller, Inc. (office furniture/Zeeland, MI) 888-646-4400 www.hermanmiller.com

HR Magazine (periodical/Alexandria, VA) 703-548-3400 www.shrm.org

Indoor Air Quality Association (industry group/Rockville, MD) 301-231-8388 www.iaqa.org

International Ergonomics Association (industry group/Rome, Italy) www.iea.cc

International Facility Management Association (industry group/ Houston, TX) 713-623-4362 www.ifma.org

International Association of Lighting Designers (industry group/ Chicago, IL) 312-527-3677 www.iald.org

International Teleworking Association and Council (industry group/ Washington, DC) 202-547-6157 www.telecommute.org

International Workplace Studies Program/Cornell University (research/Ithaca, NY) 607-255-1950 iwsp.human.cornell.edu

Journal of Architectural Engineering (periodical/Reston, VA) 703-295-6290 http://scitation.aip.org/aeo/

Journal of Interior Design (periodical) www.ejid.org

Knoll, Inc. (office furniture/East Greenville, PA) 800-343-5665 www.knoll.com

Lighting Research Center/Rensselaer Polytechnic Institute (research/Troy, NY) 518-687-7100 www.lrc.rpi.edu

Metropolis Magazine (periodical/New York, NY) 212-627-9977 www.metropolismag.com

National Association of Industrial and Office Properties (industry group/Herndon, VA) 703-904-7100 www.naiop.org

National Building Museum (research, information/ Washington, DC) 202-272-2448 www.nbm.org

National Institute for Occupational Safety and Health/Centers for Disease Control & Prevention/U.S. HHS (government resource/ Washington, DC) 202-401-6997 www.cdc.gov/niosh/homepage.html

National Lighting Bureau (industry group/Silver Spring, MD) 301-587-9572 www.nlb.org

National Real Estate Investor (periodical/New York, NY) 212-462-3588 www.nreionline.com

Occupational Health & Safety Administration/U.S. Department of Labor (government resource/Washington, DC) 800-321-6742 www.osha.gov

Office of Real Property/U.S. General Services Administration (government resource/Washington, DC) 202-501-0856 www.gsa.gov

Rocky Mountain Institute (research/Snowmass, CO) 970-927-3851 www.rmi.org

Smart Communities Network/U.S. DOE (government resource) www.sustainable.doe.gov

Society of Industrial and Office Realtors (industry group/Washington, DC) 202449-8200 www.sior.com

Steelcase, Inc. (office furniture/Grand Rapids, MI) 616-247-2710 www.steelcase.com

Urban Land Institute (industry group/Washington, DC) 202-624-7000 www.uli.org

U. S. Green Building Council (standards, certification/Washington, DC) 202-828-5100 www.usgbc.org

Windows and Daylighting Group/Lawrence Berkeley National Laboratory (research/Berkeley, CA) 510-486-5064 http://windows.lbl.gov

Workforce (periodical/Irvine, CA) 949-255-5340 www.workforce.com

Bibliography

Abdou, Ossama A. "Effects of Luminous Environment on Worker Productivity in Building Spaces." *Journal of Architectural Engineering*, September 1997.

American Society of Interior Designers. "Productive Workplaces: How Design Increases Productivity, Expert Insights." 1998, ASID.

—. "Sound Solutions: Increasing Office Productivity Through Integrated Acoustic Planning and Noise Reduction Strategies." 1996, ASID.

—. "Productive Workplaces: How Design Increases Productivity." 1998, ASID.

—. "Workplace Values: How Employees Want to Work." ASID.

Anderson, Katherine. "Alternative Officing: Revolution or Merely Redesign?" *Journal of Property Management*, January 1995.

Aronoff, Stan; Kaplan, Audrey. *Total Workplace Performance: Rethinking the Office Environment*. 1995, WDL Publications.

Barber, Christine. "Brave New Workplace." *Facilities Design & Management*, April 2001.

Barling, Julian; Frone, Michael R. *The Psychology of Workplace Safety*. 2004, American Psychological Association.

Becker, Franklin; Quinn, Kristen L.; Rappaport, Andrew J.; Sims, William R. *Implementing Innovative Workplaces: Organizational Implications of Different Strategies*. 1994, New York State College of Human Ecology and International Workplace Studies Program/Cornell University.

—. *New Working Practices: Benchmarking Flexible Scheduling, Staffing, and Work Location in an International Context*. 1993, International Workplace Studies Program/Cornell University.

Becker, Franklin; Sims, William. *Offices That Work: Balancing Communication, Flexibility and Cost*. 2001, International Workplace Studies Program/Cornell University.

Becker, Franklin; Sims, William; Davis, Bethany. *Managing Space Efficiently.* 1991, International Facility Management Program/Cornell University.

Becker, Franklin; Steele, Fritz. *Workplace by Design: Mapping the High-Performance Workscape.* 1995, Jossey-Bass, Publishers.

Becker, Franklin; Tennessen, Carolyn M.; Dahl, Lisa M. *Managing Workplace Change.* 1997, International Workplace Studies Program/Cornell University.

Bencivenga, Dominic. "A Humanistic Approach to Space." *HR Magazine*, March 1998.

Boyce, Peter; Hunter, Claudia; Howlett, Owen. "The Benefits of Daylight through Windows." 2003, Lighting Research Center/Rensselaer Polytechnic Institute.

Brand, Stewart. *How Buildings Learn: What Happens After They're Built.* 1994, Viking Penguin.

Brill, Michael. *Using Office Design to Increase Productivity.* 1984, Workplace Design and Productivity, Inc.

Building Owners and Managers Association (BOMA) International Foundation. "Integrated Systems: Increasing Building and Workplace Performance." 2000, BOMA International Foundation.

BOMA International and the Urban Land Institute. "What Office Tenants Want: Office Tenant Survey Report." 1999, BOMA International, the Urban Land Institute.

Cascio, Wayne F. "Managing a Virtual Workplace." *Academy of Management Executives,* August 2000.

Chapman, Robert E. "Benefits and Costs of Research: A Case Study of Cybernetic Building Systems." Office of Applied Economics/National Instutute of Standards and Technology, 1999.

Chen, Allan; Vine, Ed. "The Costs of Indoor Air Quality Illnesses: An Insurance Loss Reduction Perspective." 1997, Office of Energy Efficiency and Renewable Energy/U.S. Department of Energy.

Croome-Gale, Derek J. *Creating the Productive Workplace.* 1999, Routledge.

Davenport, Tom. "Big Offices are Better." *CIO*, September 1, 2003.

DYG, Inc. "The Second Bottom Line: Competing for Talent Using Innovative Workplace Design." 1998, Knoll, Inc.

Environmental Protection Agency. "Energy Cost and IAQ Performance of Ventilation Systems and Controls." Indoor Environments Division/Office of Air and Radiation/U. S. EPA, 2000.

Federal Facilities Council Staff. *Learning from Our Buildings: A State-of-the-Practice Summary of Post-Occupancy Evaluation*. 2001, National Academies Press.

Fitz-Enz, Jac. *ROI of Human Capital: Measuring the Economic Value of Employee Performance*. 2000, AMACOM.

Fredrickson, Jack M. *Cost Reduction in the Office*. 1984, AMACOM.

Gabriel, Richard F. *What Managers and Engineers Should Know about Human Factors*. 2003, SAE.

Harris, David A.; Engen, Byron W.; Fitch, William E. (editors). *Planning and Designing the Office Environment*, 2nd edition. 1991, Van Nostrand Reinhold.

Herman Miller. "Beyond Four Walls and a Door: Understanding Privacy in the Office." 2003, Herman Miller, Inc.

—. "Cross Performance at Work: What New Roles Mean to Chairs We Sit In." 2001, Herman Miller, Inc.

—. "Experience of Color." 2001, Herman Miller, Inc.

—. "The Impact of Churn: Making Workplace Assets." 2003, Herman Miller, Inc.

—. "It's Here Somewhere: The Effects of Storage Methods on Job Performance." 2003, Herman Miller, Inc.

—. "It's a Matter of Balance: New Understandings of Open Plan Acoustics." 2002, Herman Miller, Inc.

—. "Lighting in the Workplace: New Priorities." 2001, Herman Miller, Inc.

—. "Making Teamwork Work: Designing Spaces that Support

Collaborative Efforts." 2002, Herman Miller, Inc.

—. "New Executive Officescapes: Moving from Private Office to Open Environments." 2003, Herman Miller, Inc.

—. "Office Alternatives: Working On-Site." 2001, Herman Miller, Inc.

—. "Office Environments: The North American Perspective." 2002, Herman Miller, Inc.

—. "Taking on Workplace Change." 2003, Herman Miller, Inc.

—. "Telecommuting: Working Off-Site." 2001, Herman Miller, Inc.

—. "Three-Dimensional Branding: Using Space as a Medium for the Message." 2003, Herman Miller, Inc.

—. "Vision and the Computerized Office." 2001, Herman Miller, Inc.

Horgen, Turid; Joroff, Michael; Porter, William L.; Schön, Donald A. *Excellence by Design: Transforming Workplace and Work Practice.* 1999, John Wiley & Sons.

Karwowski, Waldemar (editor). *International Encyclopedia of Ergonomics and Human Factors.* 2001, Taylor & Francis.

Kroemer, Karl; Kroemer, Anne. *Office Ergonomics.* 2001, Taylor & Francis.

Lawrence, Peter. "Building Design: More Than Meets the Eye." *Journal of Business Strategy*, July 1989.

Lister, Debra Brinegar; Jenicek, Elisabeth M. "Productivity and Indoor Environmental Conditions Research: An Annotated Bibliography for Facility Engineers." 1998, U.S. Army Corps of Engineers.

Maas, Michael. "The Productivity Value of Environment." *Mangement Review*, March, 1983.

Macleod, Dan. *The Rules of Work.* 2000, Taylor & Francis.

Mahnke, Frank H. *Color, Environment, and Human Response.* 1996, John Wiley & Sons.

Managing Office Technology. "Too Much Togetherness." *Managing Office Technology*, September 1998.

Marmot, Alexi; Eley, Joanna. *Office Space Planning: Designing for Tomorrow's Workplace*. 2000, McGraw-Hill.

Matthes, Karen. "Rx for Healthier Offices." *Management Review*, September 1992.

Morrow, Wayne. "Personal Environments and Productivity in the Intelligent Building." 1995, Intelligent Building Institute Intellibuild 95.

Myerson, Jeremy; Ross, Philip. *The Creative Office*. 1999, Gingko Press.

Noyes, Jan. *Designing for Humans*. 2001, Psychology Press.

Pekala, Nancy. "Cubicles Be Gone!" *Journal of Property Management*, September 2001.

Rappoport, James; Cushman, Robert F.; Daroff, Karen (editors). *Office Planning and Design Desk Reference*. 1991, Interscience.

Raymond, Santa; Cunliffe, Roger. *Tomorrow's Office: Creating Effective and Humane Interiors*. 2000, E. & FN Spon/Taylor & Francis Group.

Ruck, Nancy C. (editor). *Building Design and Human Performance*. 1989, Van Nostrand Reinhold.

Sassone, Peter G. "Office Productivity: The Impacts of Staffing, Intellectual Specialization, and Technology." *Technology Analysis & Stragetic Management*, Vol. 8, Number 3, 1996.

Seppänen, O.A.; Fisk, W.J.; Mendell, M.J. "Association of Ventilation Rates and CO_2-Concentratons with Health and Other Responses in Commercial and Industrial Buildings." *Indoor Air*, 1999, 9:226-252.

Sheedy, J.E. "Vision Problems at VDTs, A Survey of Optometrists." 1991, VDT Eye Clinic/U.C. Berkeley and Optical Coating Lavoratory, Inc.

Shoshkes, Lila. *Space Planning: Designing the Office Environment*. 1976, Architectural Record Books.

Shumake, M. Glynn. *Increasing Productivity and Profit in the Workplace: A Guide to Office Planning and Design.* 1992, John Wiley & Sons.

Smith, Phyl; Kearny, Lynn. *Creating Workplaces Where People Can Think.* 1994, Jossey-Bass, Publishers.

Steelcase. "Assessing Workplace Intangibles." 2000, Steelcase, Inc.

—. "HotHouse Environments: Fostering Breakthrough Innovations." 2001, Steelcase, Inc.

—. "Measuring Business Results." 2000, Steelcase, Inc.

Steele, Fritz. *Making and Managing High-Quality Workplaces: An Organizational Ecology.* 1986, Teachers College Press.

Strasser, Helmut; Gruen, Kristina; Koch, Werner. *Occupational Ergonomics.* 1999/2000, IOS Press.

Teicholz, Eric. *Facility Design & Mangement Handbook.* 2001, McGraw-Hill.

Vischer, Jacqueline C. *Environmental Quality in Offices.* 1989, Van Nostrand Reinhold.

Wah, Louisa. "The Power Office." *Management Review*, May 1998.

Wineman, Jean D. (editor). *Behavioral Issues in Office Design.* 1986, Van Nostrand Reinhold.

Appendix

The Myth of the Hawthorne Effect

Between 1924 and 1933, the Hawthorne Works, a manufacturing facility run by the Western Electric Company in Hawthorne, Illinois, was the site of an ongoing series of experiments studying productivity. One phase of this research was conducted by Elton Mayo and a team from the Harvard Business School, who created a novel series of controlled environments which were intended to provide accurate measurements of output under varying conditions.

Mayo used different schemes to influence output for a small group of carefully-selected workers. He varied the number and duration of breaks, the length of the work day, the availability of a free hot meal, pay linked to piece work, and other factors, and relied on attentive supervision to monitor and control the work activity.

With no exceptions, the use of any variable produced the same results, a measurable increase in productivity, even after the variables had been discontinued. The prevailing conclusion from this experiment, still popular among some experts today, is that a sympathetic, friendly management style and close teamwork among workers who bond will lead to improved performance.

However, this conclusion does not represent what really happened. Reexaminations of this classic experiment indicate that the work environment itself was a critical factor in determining the results. The test group of workers was isolated from their normal place on the factory floor and all of the workers selected were experienced and well-motivated to perform, at least initially.

In the isolated, comfortable test space, the subjects were free to converse and choose who they worked next to, factors missing from the manufacturing plant. This, as well as the various incentives used, was enough to initially improve morale and productivity. But when two workers — 40 percent of the total group — began to slack off, lowering overall productivity, the researchers replaced them with hand-picked substitutes with more appropriate motivation.

The supervising style also shifted. The original sympathetic interaction was deliberately replaced by harsher methods and pressure tactics, which were used to overcome the obstacles represented by the slackers. When the two underperforming workers were replaced and productivity shot up, the management style reverted to a more positive, friendly form. Conclusions published about this experiment emphasized only the connection between the supportive management style and a cooperative team effort with the increase in output. For decades, the Hawthorne Effect has been hailed as an exemplary workplace experiment emphasizing the need to give workers more autonomy and encourage softer management tactics.

Even though follow-up studies failed to replicate these findings, the myth lives on. Contemporary research in the work environment makes a strong case for the appropriateness of supportive managers but attributes most gains in productivity to other factors, including incentives, better communications between workers, and healthy working environments.

Impact of Productivity

What is the cost difference between leasing secondhand space and a User Effective™ Workplace? The cost to lease an existing 50,000 square foot space at $16/square foot is $800,000 per year. By comparison, consider the cost for a build-to-suit structure of the same size at roughly $20/square foot, a total of $1 million, 25 percent higher than the $16/square foot lease rate.

But that's not the whole picture. Assume a 50,000 square foot building built at $20/square foot has 250 employees at an average annual salary per employee of $50,000, providing an average of 200 square feet per employee. Based on the expected improvements that a custom-built office provides, the higher cost of the new space comes with a bonus. Every 1 percent gain in productivity by the staff produces a $125,000 gain.

GAIN IN PRODUCTIVITY	ANNUAL SAVINGS	SAVINGS PER SQ.FT.	REAL COST PER SQ.FT.
0%	—	—	$20.00
1%	$125,000	$ 2.50	$17.50
2%	$250,000	$5.00	$15.00
3%	$375,000	$7.50	$12.50
4%	$500,000	$10.00	$10.00
5%	$625,000	$12.50	$7.50
6%	$750,000	$15.00	$5.00
7%	$875,000	$17.50	$2.50
8%	$1,000,000	$20.00	—
9%	$1,125,000	$22.50	—
10%	$1,250,000	$25.00	—

Evaluating the Use of Space

Organizations can measure and analyze their use of space using a variety of methods. This includes prepared surveys and interactive tools, prepared guidelines and questionaires, and interviews with those involved in a use study. Some interactive tools and prepared forms are available from vendors, professional groups, and books, and consultants who specialize in this kind of work are also available.

In general, the process of acquiring information should provide three types of answers:

1. **Descriptive**. Factual, literal definitions or measurements of space, fixtures, or activities.

2. **Evaluative**. Personal assessment of functionality, comfort, or satisfaction.

3. **Projective**. Personal ideas of what is needed or desired.

The categories used to define work spaces include:

Size/layout of workspace
- physical measurements
- user-perceived limits of personal space
- description of enclosure panels/walls/doors
- space configuration
- location relative to office fixtures/windows/access
- comfort level
- satisfaction level

Furniture/fixtures of workspace
- seating
- desks/work surfaces
- storage

197

- work and personal display space
- flexibility
- personal modifications
- comfort level
- satisfaction level

Use of equipment
- number and type of equipment used
- purpose/frequency/duration of use
- location/access of equipment used
- shared equipment
- comfort level
- satisfaction level

Workspace environment
- noise factors
- air quality
- lighting quality
- room temperature
- level of control over noise/air/light/temperature
- electrical/network service access
- interior access/circulation
- security
- safety
- maintenance/repairs
- window access
- comfort level
- satisfaction level

Design/appeal of workspace
- color/materials/surfacing
- statement of status/hierarchy
- art/design details

Privacy and interaction
- speech
- noise distraction
- visual distraction
- visibility
- control over distractions/privacy
- shared space
- features that simplify/encourage communication
- comfort level
- satisfaction level

Structures have their own set of factors in addition to the above. The general amount of space available for use must be considered, as well as the various subcategories of use. Engineers and architects typically have to make the decisions about support systems covered by building codes, such as HVAC, alarms, rest rooms, doorways, garages, etc., although this may include some practical input from the tenant.

The division and placement of workspaces and shared facilities require the most care because these have the greatest impact on communications, privacy, and the use of space. As with workspace surveys, quantitative and qualitative input can help evaluate the adequacy of existing meeting space, board rooms, private offices, open office plans, break rooms, filing rooms, and other spaces.

Exterior evaluations are also appropriate, as they help determine the value of building facades, landscaping, parking areas, public access, and other factors that have an impact on the health and effectiveness of an organization.

Index

203

207

The Aardex Corporation

Founded in 1983, Aardex Corporation is a one-stop real estate development firm specializing in build-to-suit, User Effective™ workplaces. Aardex provides a single point of contact for its clients, with accountability for the entire design and construction process. We have in-house expertise in contracting, design, financing, project management, and property management.

By incorporating all these resources under one roof, we reduce the time and cost to develop workplaces. These efficiencies are reflected in our bids, often millions of dollars lower than the next one, and Aardex clients report an added bonus, productivity gains of up to 30 percent.

Our design and construction projects have focused on energy savings, reduction in construction waste, cost-efficient utility usage, environmentally-supportive building materials, and healthy indoor work environments. As an early adopter of the principles of "building green," Aardex is an active participant in the sustainability movement, including the LEED™ program from the U.S. Green Building Council.

We are committed to best practices that nurture a sustainable earth with prosperous inhabitants.

Aardex Corporation
Denver, Colorado 303-987-9000
www.aardex.com